BOOST YOUR RETIREMENT INCOME NOW!

What you can do now to increase the value of your 401(k) and IRA accounts

David Rye

Western Publications
10271 South 175ᵗʰ Avenue
Goodyear, AZ 85358-5502

CONTENTS

6

Introduction

Retirement is on the way for every baby boomer in America. How your finances stack up by the time you retire will go a long way toward determining the sort of retirement you will be able to enjoy. Unfortunately, far too many of us approach retirement ill-prepared. Either we've simply not saved enough or what we have managed to put away has been invested in the wrong places. And many of us ignore the issue of planning for retirement completely.

Whether you are 50 or older, you will feel the effects of the Age Wave. Even those who already are retired have been affected by it. Although many of the changes will be positive, not everyone will enjoy riding the wave. You have to prepare for the consequences of the new trends that have in part brought about by the collapse of the housing market in 2008, a vicious bear market in 2009, and the worst recession this country has seen since the Great Depression that followed.

Fortunately, Americans have an uncanny ability to foresee and adapt to changes. Most of the financial disasters or near disasters of the past did not have the severe adverse consequences that were predicted at the onset. This book is designed to address the many challenges of retiring. Starting with the basics, we'll walk you through every important element that pertains to building a financially solid retirement plan. Along the way, we offer tips and advice to help you check to make certain you remain on track with your 401(k) and IRA accounts. We address just how much money you'll need to enjoy the retirement you wish, along with savings and investment strategies to help you reach your financial goals.

We'll also discuss other important elements needed to achieve a secure retirement, including health and long-term care insurance, housing, the cost of living, and Social Security. You'll learn about many options pertaining to retirement that you may not have considered before. We encourage you, with the help of this book, to become pro-active in planning for your retirement. The earlier you start thinking about your retirement, the more fulfilling your retirement is likely to be. With this book in your hands, you've taken a critical first step toward that objective.

Chapter 1

Wave Watching

Don't just look at the wave. Whatever you do, prepare yourself for the ride!

The age wave is coming and nothing can stop it. It will transform the future of virtually every American's retirement lifestyle. We have already seen changes in health care, housing, the financial markets, and pension programs. Because of key, unstoppable trends that are already are in place, changes in the coming years in these and other areas affecting retirement will continue. We don't know if the best-case or worst-case scenarios or something in between will have on individual retirees. We do know that you must be alert to the possibility of additional changes in the future and to be ready to adapt to them.

Those who retired not many years ago would be shocked by the task faced by the Baby Boomers, that generation of 76 million people born between 1946 and 1964 who are retiring in the early twenty-first century. Many of the retirement issues to be addressed today weren't even on the radar screen in the past. Those who retired in the 1960s through the 1990s developed the image of retirement that many Americans still hold today. They retired at age 65 with company pensions, solid investments, and paid-off mortgages. Soaring real estate values enabled many of them to sell their homes for tremendous profits. With the advent of the twenty first century, that has all changed.

What to Do Now

Many boomers had made what they thought were good investments saw a significant drop in the value of their 401(k) and IRA accounts in 2008 and well into 2010. The graph that follows shows what happened to the average price of a stock on the New York and NASDQ stock exchanges from March of 2008 through March of 2009 when the "Big Wave" hit the market. If you're willing to take the time to really get to know what's inside your 401(k) and IRA accounts, then you can start growing it into a nest egg that will help you retire comfortably.

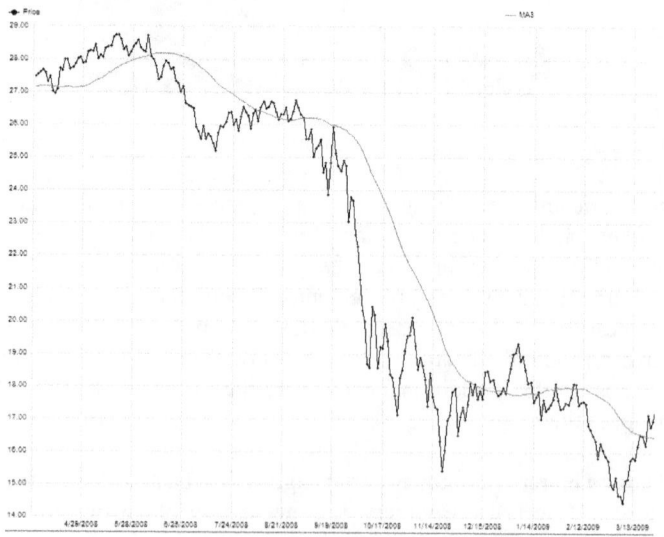

The Big Wave

It doesn't matter how young or old you are. Even if you're on the verge of retirement, you still should be invested in a mix of assets that is providing you with a decent rate of return. Why? Life fortunately doesn't stop after you leave the company's retirement party. You could still have thirty or more years of the good life ahead of you if you can afford it. If your 401(k) or IRA is just creeping along, it will get devoured by inflation. Your retirement accounts are powerful retirement weapons in your retirement arsenal.

Gone are the days when retirement by definition meant bingo, bland food, and a level of general inactivity that slowly slipped toward physical and mental erosion. Retirees are doing everything these days, from traveling to starting a business to returning to school to finish a degree or work on a new one. But alongside those advantages have come a new set of challenges. First, one of the foremost issues is longevity since we're all living longer; we all have to be able to afford that longer life span. It's a simple fact-the longer you live, the more expensive it's likely going to be.

Fortunately, the financial element of retirement isn't nearly as automatic or as out of our hands as it used to be. Not too long ago, Social Security and company pension plans developed, managed, and funded exclusively by your employer were the financial bedrock for many retirees. You worked, the money was put away for you automatically and, one day, you hung up your working shoes and started receiving monthly checks.

Now, with the advent of defined contribution plans where you're the one making the financial calls, the issue of how successful a retirement you were able to enjoy has been placed squarely in our laps. Add to that the exploding number of self-employed people and the spread of personal savings vehicles such as Individual Retirement Accounts, and the question of how to map out and execute a successful retirement funding program is placed directly on your shoulders more so than any other generation. Your first proactive effort should be to get to know everything you can about your retirement accounts so that you can prepare a plan of action.

How 401(k) Plans Work

Employer sponsored 401(k) plans are retirement savings plans that were created by the Internal Revenue Service in 1978. It lets you put some of your income away now to use later when you need it for retirement. The federal government in its infinite wisdom, created tax breaks for 401(k) participants as an incentive to motivate people to start saving for retirement.

The plans rapidly grew in popularity when employees discovered that the plans allowed their employers to make tax-sheltered contributions directly into their 401(k) accounts. They also liked the fact that 401(k) plans were more portable than conventional pension plans in that they could easily be moved from one employer to the next. Employers liked them too because they were less expensive than defined-benefit retirement plans to fund and were easier to administer.

When you elect to participate in your employer's 401(k) program, you must agree to deposit into the plan some amount of money you determine from your paycheck. Some employer will match all or a part of your contribution. You don't pay federal income tax on contributions until you withdraw your money. What your 401(k) will be worth when you retire depends on three basic factors: how much you and your employer contributed into the plan, what rate of return you realized from the investments you made, and the length of time your money remained in the plan before you withdrew it.

The Employee Retirement Income Security Act (ERISA) is the federal law that sets the standards for employee retirement plans including 401(k). Employers are required to provide to their employees documentation that describes the daily operation and benefits of their 401(k) plan, identifies the trust fund that holds their employees' account, and keeps them up to date on their account balance, deposits, and earnings.

12

How Conventional IRAs Work

Basically, an Independent Retirement Account more commonly known as an IRA is a savings vehicle with added advantages. It allows you to save money on a tax-deferred basis for your retirement. An IRA is exceedingly simple to set up. You can still do it with as little as a single-page form or you can now establish IRA accounts online in a matter of minutes. When you first open an IRA, you may assume that you've made a lifelong friend. And, in a sense your IRA will be with you throughout your working life and, from there, doing its financial bit to help finance your retirement. But that's not to say that where you keep an IRA is always going to remain the same. If, for instance, you were working with a financial planner or broker who has moved on to another firm, you may wish to follow him or her. Likewise, if you were disappointed in their performance, find someone with greater potential.

They've been around since 1981, providing a solid vehicle with which to build a financial base for retirement. For many people planning for retirement, an IRA is a key component of their retirement plan. IRAs now are essential to the retirement plans of many Americans. IRA owners need to know how to take maximum advantage of these accounts, keep up with the ever changing rules, and learn how to avoid some of the traps of IRA ownership. They also should consider some strategies that are counterintuitive. Sometimes these unconventional moves can increase the benefits from IRAs and other tax-deferred accounts.

One of the best features of an IRA is its flexibility. Once you have money in an account, you can pretty much do what you want with it, at least from an allocation point of view. You can invest in mutual funds, stocks, bonds, money markets-there's a broad range of options from which to choose. You can even opt for a managed IRA fund, which, over time, automatically shifts its investment mix as you near retirement. There are other advantages as well. Depending on your circumstances, you may be able to deduct your contribution (more about this in Chapter 9). And no matter if the contribution is deductible or not, your money grows on a tax-deferred basis until you begin to withdraw it after you retire.

Deductibility is by no means an IRA's sole advantage. Contribution levels have been similarly increased. From the initial $2,000 limit, you can now contribute as much as $5,000 to an IRA (see the following table). Although deductibility is, needless to say, an attractive element of IRAs, you should strongly consider opening one up and contributing to it on a regular basis. One reason, among others, is the IRA's tax-deferred status, which lets you save and earn interest on money in an IRA with no tax impact until you begin withdrawing the money. The thinking here is that when you retire, you will likely be in a lower tax bracket than when you were working and hence, less of a tax bite on the withdrawals.

2010 IRA Deduction Schedule		
Filing Status	Adjusted Gross Income Limits	Amount of Deduction
Single or Head of Household and you are covered by a retirement plan at work	$53,000 or less	Full deduction
	$53,001 to $63,000	Partial deduction
	$63,001 or more	No deduction
Married filing jointly and spouse has a retirement plan at work	$159,000 or less	Full deduction
	$159,001 to $169,000	Partial deduction
	$169,001 or more	No deduction
Single or Head of Household and you are NOT covered by a retirement plan at work	Any amount	Full deduction
Married filing jointly and spouse DOES NOT have a retirement plan at work	Any amount	Full deduction
Consult IRS Publication 590 at www.irs.gov for specific IRA rules and questions		

IRA contributions are a do-it-or-lose-it proposition. If you don't make a contribution in a given year, you can't make it up in the following tax year. You're allowed to contribute up to $5,000 a year or $6,000 a year if you are 50 or older. You can deduct your IRA contribution if you meet certain income restrictions that are covered in the table that follows. The income limits are base on the amount of your adjusted gross income (AGI) that is the sum of your work income added to any other income you had such as interest and dividends from investments.

You can withdraw money from your IRA any time you want, but the IRS will apply a 10 percent penalty on unqualified withdrawals. You are allowed to take qualified withdrawals if you are 59½ or older, are disabled, use your withdrawal to pay for college or other qualified educational expense, or withdraw up to $10,000 to pay for a first-time home purchase. All or a portion of withdrawals are taxed at your income tax rate in the year you took the withdrawal. You must begin to take withdrawals following the year you turn 70½.

How Roth IRAs Work

In the 1990s, Congress unveiled a new version of the IRA that became known as the Roth IRA. Roth IRAs provides some potentially attractive alternative features to the conventional IRA. For one thing, singles making up to $110,000 a year or couples as high as $159,000 could qualify to open a Roth. Conventional IRAs and Roths share many common features. Both provide tax free growth for whatever money you invest in them. Both allow complete freedom for you to choose the investment that actually makes up your IRA account. That can be stocks, bonds, mutual funds or whatever you like that best serves your investment goals. You are also free to adjust your investment mix to reflect any changes in your risk tolerance or objectives.

Congress went a step further and allowed many people a chance to convert their regular IRAs to Roth IRAs. It doesn't matter if the regular IRA contributions were made because the owner was unaware of the Roth's advantages or was not eligible to make Roth contributions. It also doesn't matter if the regular IRA was opened before the Roth IRA was created in 1997 or as a result of rolling over a 401(k) or other retirement plan into the IRA. The IRA can be deductible or nondeductible. In any of these cases, the IRA owner might be able to convert the regular IRA into a Roth IRA. In addition, the IRA owner can choose to convert the entire IRA or any portion of it into a Roth IRA.

The primary difference between a conventional IRA and the Roth IRA is in tax treatment. While you may be able to deduct conventional IRA contributions, a Roth offers no up-front deductibility. However, proceeds from a Roth may be withdrawn tax-free after you retire whereas a conventional IRA is taxed. Another benefit of the Roth IRA is that the owner has better access to funds. Loans still are not allowed. The Roth IRA owner, however, can withdraw contributions made to the account tax free and penalty free at any time. Owners of other IRAs and 401(k) do not have that level of access to their money. You're eligible to participate in a Roth if your adjusted gross income falls within the ranges in the following table:

2010 Roth IRA Deduction Schedule		
Filing Status	**Adjusted Gross Income**	**Amount of Deduction**
Married, filing jointly or head of household	Up to $159,000	Full deduction
	$159,001 to $169,000	Declining deduction
Single	Up to $101,000	Full deduction
	$101,000 to $116,000	Declining deduction
Married filing separately	Up to $10,000	Declining deduction
Consult IRS Publication 590 at www.irs.gov for specific IRA rules and questions		

There is no tax benefit for making a contribution to the Roth IRA. The contribution is made with after-tax dollars. The eventual benefits of the Roth IRA, however, are substantial. The income and capital gains compound tax free as with a regular IRA. When distributions are made, they are free of income taxes if the distributions are made more than five years after the first contributions to the IRA and after the owner is age 59. In addition, unlike other IRAs, the owner of a Roth IRA is not required to begin taking required minimum distributions after reaching age 70. The owner can let the income and gains compound as long as desired. A beneficiary who inherits a Roth IRA must begin required minimum distributions, but the distributions can be scheduled based on the beneficiary's age. Also unlike a conventional IRA, an owner can make contributions to a Roth IRA after age 70.

A Roth IRA has the same annual contribution limit as conventional IRAs. The different types of IRAs potentially compound to the same amount over the years. With distributions from the Roth IRA being free of income taxes, the after-tax value of the Roth IRA far exceeds the value of a conventional IRA. Even if the tax savings from a deductible IRA are invested separately, the Roth IRA usually will generate more after-tax wealth.

However, not everyone is eligible to open a Roth IRA. There are income limits, as with deductible IRAs. Anyone whose adjusted gross income exceeds the limits cannot open a Roth IRA. In 2003, single taxpayers had their ability to make Roth IRA contributions phased out at adjusted incomes between $95,000 and $110,000. For married taxpayers filing jointly, the phase out occurred between $150,000 and $160,000.

Which IRA is Right for You?

Now that you're inundated with information about conventional and Roth IRAs, which one should you choose if you have no IRA at all at this point? Like so many things to do with planning for retirement, there's really no hard-and-fast answer, as both choices offer advantages and potential drawbacks.

If you're eligible to take the tax deduction afforded by the conventional IRA, the decision to switch to a Roth becomes a bit problematic. On the one hand, no one would blame you for grabbing the up-front tax break. On the other hand, if your income now is too high to take the conventional IRA deduction, you're better off opting for the Roth. If nothing else, a tax break at the end of the retirement cycle is better than no tax break at all.

Roths may be a better choice due to their greater flexibility come retirement. As we pointed out earlier, there is no mandatory withdrawal provision, which is great for people planning on living a long time who want to have the greatest amount of leeway with their savings. And, Roths are a great way to pass money on to others unlike conventional IRAs, which are not inheritance friendly. Roths also offer tax advantages other than the ones we've covered. In some instances, a great deal of taxable income after retirement such as that from conventional IRAs can cause your Social Security benefits to be taxed as well. The tax-free withdrawal provisions of the Roth mitigate this

If you have a conventional IRA in place that you've funded to the maximum and you've heard about all the wonderful benefits afforded by the Roth, what should you do? Should you take the plunge and convert your old IRA to a Roth? On the surface, the prospect seems to be a no-brainer. In effect, you're opting out of a taxed program for an alternative where every penny you withdraw after you retire is tax-free. If you choose to roll over a conventional IRA into a Roth, you will have to pay taxes on whatever you move to the new account-more concern.

If you open an IRA and expect to access the money within five years or less, go with the conventional IRA. Roths' five-year withdrawal penalty window will only force you to take a needless hit. There are also income limitations. Currently, if your adjusted gross income is greater than $100,000 in the year you want to convert, you're not allowed to change from a conventional IRA to a Roth. Specifically, on any contributions and earnings that were either tax-deductible or tax deferred. In a way, it is understandable if you got a deduction on everything you put into a conventional IRA and want to move it into a Roth to gain tax-free access after retirement, it's something of a double dip.

If you anticipate being in a higher tax bracket after retiring, take the tax hit now and convert-better a tax slap now than a tax wallop later. Also, it's a good choice if you have a nondeductible IRA that hasn't grown that much in value-perhaps one you started a couple of years ago and that has pretty much languished where it is. If that's the case, your taxes will likely be light and, from there, you can enjoy all the pluses of a Roth.

The key here is to let your custodian know that you intend to take the proceeds and, rather than just pocketing them, put them into another IRA account. You're letting your custodian know not to withhold any taxes. The other key is the federally mandated time frame. You have 60 days to put the money into a new IRA account. Fail to do that, and you will be required to pay a penalty to the IRS. Also pay attention to rollover limitations. The IRS only allows you one rollover per account every 12 months. Even if you roll over only a portion of assets within a particular IRA account, the remaining funds can't be touched for 12 calendar months.

The transfer option is often the easiest and safest means of moving IRA funds. Simply instruct your current IRA custodian to transfer the funds directly to another custodian. In this fashion, you never take possession of the money in any way, which eliminates concern over the 60-day limit with rollovers. This also eliminates the 12-month rollover limitation, so, theoretically at least, you can execute transfers as often as you like.

Converting IRAs

There are two requirements for converting a conventional IRA into a Roth IRA. First, taxes on the IRA must be paid as though the amount converted were distributed to the taxpayer. For example, suppose there is a deductible conventional IRA with a balance of $100,000. If the owner decides to convert the entire amount, then $100,000 must be included in gross income in the year of the conversion. If $50,000 is converted, then $50,000 is included in gross income. If the IRA has nondeductible contributions, then the conversion of the nondeductible contributions is not taxed.

Second, the adjusted gross income on your tax return for the year cannot exceed $100,000 excluding any IRA conversion amount that is included in gross income. The IRA owner's filing status doesn't matter. The $100,000 limit is the same whether the taxpayer is married filing jointly, single, or head of household. This means that each spouse's income is counted as the other spouse's income when determining the income limit. If one spouse earns over $100,000, neither spouse will be able to convert an IRA as long as they are married, regardless of the other spouse's income level. If the taxpayer is married filing separately, the income limit is $0. In other words, a conversion is not possible unless the taxpayer has no other income at all. The rules are simple. The trick is determining when it makes sense to incur the cost of converting an ordinary IRA into a Roth IRA. The answer depends on several factors. The IRA owner has to make assumptions about these factors and compare the results of continuing to own the conventional IRA with converting to a Roth IRA. The more money that is left inside the IRA to benefit from tax-free compounding, the more advantageous it is' to convert to a Roth IRA.

Where to Invest Funds

One of the beauties of IRAs is their inherent flexibility with regard to where you put the money you invest in them. Unlike other retirement vehicles, IRAs are just about wide open to most any sort of retirement choice. You can choose individual stocks, mutual funds, bonds, certificates of deposit, even something as rock-solid conservative as a conventional savings account. That range of choice can actually set up another boondoggle with regard to your IRA specifically, where you should put your money and, as a result, just how aggressive you should be. Some people may opt for a more conservative route, choosing stable investments such as CDs or money market funds. Their thinking is that an IRA can be a stable backstop to an overall retirement plan (i.e., keep the money safe).

To others, IRAs are an ideal choice for more aggressive options, such as stocks and mutual funds. With a possible long-term time frame facing them before they expect to access funds for retirement, their feeling is that an IRA is the best place to roll the dice a bit. There are two major prohibitions with regard to IRAs. One is collectibles, including art, stomps, antiques, and other like items. You may also not invest in real estate you own, such as your own home or rental property.

There's no right or wrong in this argument. It does illustrate the range of choice you have with your IRA and in turn, how critical it is to gauge the right investment approach for you.
In this chapter, we'll introduce you to a variety of retirement funding vehicles. We'll provide a quick overview of their various features, their advantages and drawbacks and how, taken individually or used as a package, they can work to build a solid financial retirement package. And, in subsequent chapters, we'll go into additional detail regarding how to invest in them, finding the sort of risk tolerance that's right for you and other issues related to using these vehicles as effectively as possible.

Using Rollovers

If you leave an employer, there are several options regarding your 401(k) account. Many employers allow the account to be maintained with them. Another option is to transfer the account to a retirement plan at your new employer, if the new employer offers a 401(k) plan. A third option is to transfer the account to an IRA, known as an IRA rollover. This option is used most frequently, and most people roll over their 401(k) to IRA at retirement. There are a couple of ways to do an IRA rollover. The employer can give the departing employee a check for the account balance. The former employee then has up to 60 days to get the entire amount deposited in an IRA.

If the deadline is not met, the entire balance is included in income for the year it was received. In addition, the employer may be required to withhold taxes equal to 20 percent of the account balance. If the entire account balance is rolled over to an IRA, the

21

employee gets a refund of the withheld taxes. To qualify, however, the employee must roll over to the IRA not only the check received from the employer but also the 20 percent that was withheld. If the employee cannot come up with that much money, the withheld amount will be included in income for the year.

The better approach is to have the former employer transfer the balance directly to an IRA custodian designated by the employee. That way, there is no withholding and the employee doesn't have to worry about the 60-day deadline. Generally, when leaving an employer it is a good idea to roll over the 401(k) balance to an IRA. The IRA is likely to have more investment options. In addition, at retirement an employer is allowed to limit the distribution options from a 401(k) plan. As we'll learn later in this chapter, an IRA can be managed to last for a long time, even after the required minimum distributions begin after age 70.

When a 401(k) or other retirement plan is rolled over into an IRA, it is a good idea to roll over the account into a new IRA instead of an existing IRA. If you decide to work for another employer, that employer might accept transfers from other 401(k) to its 401(k). Such a transfer can be made from an IRA rollover account only if the rollover account contains only the proceeds from a previous employer's plan. If the IRA also contains other contributions, then none of the IRA can be transferred to a new employer's 401(k).

Watch Out for Inflation

The United States has been blessed with declining inflation in the years since 1982.The dramatic decline in inflation began at a time when many were forecasting that high inflation was a permanent part of America's future. There are several explanations for the decline in inflation. International monetary authorities became more educated about the dangers of inflation and how an increasing money supply leads to inflation. As a result, they became more vigilant about preventing inflation than they were prior to the 1970s.

Also, the emergence of a truly global economy put a natural lid on prices as companies had to compete with goods and services from all over the world, not just from their own countries. Production in low-wage countries kept prices down worldwide. Technology, competition, and more efficient work methods also combined to increase productivity. This higher productivity allowed businesses to produce more goods and services at lower costs, which holds down prices and inflation.

Some analysts, however, point to demographics as a key to disinflation. They say that since World War II, there has been a close relationship between inflation and the percentage of younger employees. A low percentage of younger workers (those under age 35) are tied to lower inflation. But a high percentage of younger workers are associated with higher inflation. The theory is that younger workers are less productive, and lower productivity leads to higher inflation. As the Boomers entered their early adult years, inflation soared. As the Boomers matured, inflation declined. If the relationship holds, then as the Boomers retire and the work force again becomes younger, inflation should increase.

An aging population usually means less robust economic growth. There are a host of reasons for this. One reason is that a higher percentage of the work force is past its peak productive years. With improvements in health care and lengthening life spans, we cannot be sure when the Boomers' productivity will peak. It is likely, however, that most Boomers will continue to work past their peak productive years. Because the Boomers will be a large portion of both the population and the work force, at some point productivity and economic growth are likely to fall as the Boomers age, unless there are offsetting factors.

Savings also are likely to decline as the Boomers age. This is because retirees generally don't increase their savings. They start to spend what they have accumulated. Reduced savings could lead to higher interest rates. Again, that usually means lower productivity and lower economic growth.

Another result of an aging population is that a lower percentage of the population will be in the work force. We will have fewer workers supporting each non-worker. Fewer workers for each non-worker typically lead to slower economic growth. That is because a higher portion of the income and taxes of each worker supports the non-workers. When there are fewer younger workers for each older non-worker, there is less wealth available for other expenditures, some of which would lead to more productivity and economic growth. Social Security and Medicare are the two most prominent programs through which younger workers support older non-workers. These programs are not funded in advance by taxes. Instead, they are essentially pay-as-you-go systems.

Taxes from those working during the Boomers' retirement years will fund payments to the Boomers. If there are fewer workers when payments to the Boomers are due, tax rates may have to be raised in order to foot the bill. Higher taxes cause lower fiscal efficiency and reduce economic growth. Payments to the older non-workers possibly might be funded with debt instead of taxes. This increased debt would occur at a time when overall savings are likely to decline. A lower national savings rate coupled with higher debt could lead to higher interest rates and inflation. The result of either higher interest rates or inflation would be slower economic growth.

Putting It All Together

IRAs and 401(k)s are one of the few investment options left that allows your investment to grow, tax-free, until you elect to withdraw some or all of the funds that are in your account. Generally, you should first contribute to employer-sponsored plans such as a 401(k) plan to enjoy their matching contributions before you consider opening an IRA account. You have a choice between managed or self-directed IRA accounts. Managed IRAs have professional managers who direct the investments on your behalf. Most mutual funds-based IRAs are managed. You pay an annual fee of about 1 percent of your holdings for this service.

The major differences between a Roth IRA and a conventional IRA are in the way in which they are funded and in the rules governing withdrawing funds from them. Roth IRAs are funded with your income dollars *after* taxes have been withdrawn. Conventional IRAs are funded with your income dollars *before* taxes have been withdrawn. Consequently, you are not taxed on any funds that you withdraw from a Roth IRA. And you can withdraw funds from a Roth IRA at any time, regardless of your age, without incurring a penalty. With a conventional IRA, you're taxed on withdrawals. This is not necessarily a bad thing, since your tax rate may be lower when you retire. Also with a conventional IRA, if you withdraw funds before you reach 59lh, you must pay a 10 percent penalty on the amount withdrawn. And you must start withdrawals from a conventional IRA by age 70.

An IRA account can offer you the flexibility than a 401(k) to manage your investment portfolio. However, some financial institutions offer IRA accounts that automatically manage your funds for you by choosing the areas to invest in. It is important to check with your financial institution to see what different plans are in place, and to learn and understand your options. Self-directed IRAs are set up so that you choose and manage the investments in your account yourself. Most brokers and mutual funds offer them. They have a small annual fee (usually $50 or less per year) and most self-directed IRAs offer a wide variety of investment options for you to consider. To open an IRA account, contact your financial institution.

Chapter 2

Setting Investment Goals

If you never make an investment, you'll never make or lose any money.

As the Baby Boomers age, they should expect circumstances that are dramatically different from those experienced by their parents. Their senior years will be dramatically longer and more vibrant. They will have to save and invest more than their parents did to bear the expenses of those extra years. The Boomers also are unlikely to realize the buoyant investment returns or receive the postretirement tax breaks their parents received to help with that burden. For many, money is a central element for a happy and fulfilling retirement. Even those who are prepared to live a rather frugal lifestyle will require some sort of nest egg (i.e., 401(k) or IRA) to pay a part of their day-to-day living expenses.

Every retiree needs to become more astute as an investor because their standard of living often depends heavily on the ability to save and invest. Although investment options are more complicated and uncertain than in the past, financial deregulation has produced many benefits. Many investments are no longer saddled with the fixed-interest-rate savings accounts of the earlier years. Many options available today can substantially increase an individual's wealth and enhance retirement if you understand more about the various investment markets.

Determining How Much You'll Need

Asking the question of how much money is enough to afford retirement is akin to asking how much air do you need to breathe. It all depends on the individual. Although the expenses involved-housing, food, and other costs may be the same, what you will need in retirement depends on a number of factors specific to you. While that may seem to make perfect sense, there are others who argue that there is a hard-and-fast barometer for gauging how much you'll need to retire.

Some may say that you'll need roughly 80 percent of your pre-retirement income to maintain the same lifestyle after you retire. Others are a bit less optimistic, pointing out the eroding influence of inflation that mandates 100 percent of pre-retirement income to live comparably after retirement. Still a third camp says that it costs you less not to have to earn a living (no commuting, business wardrobe, and the like). That means you can be reasonably comfortable on a mere 60 percent of what you earn now.

Don't overlook infrequent expenses such as home maintenance and improvements, appliance replacement, automobiles, travel, and help for family members. For these expenses, divide the estimated annual spending by 12 to determine a monthly amount in the budget. Suppose you plan to buy a new car every four years at a cost of $30,000. At 3 percent inflation, the cost after the first four years is about $34,000. You could set aside $708 per month in the budget to ensure having accumulated $34,000 after four years. A more sophisticated approach is to assume some interest will be earned on the fund. At 3 percent annual interest, the monthly amount to set aside would be about $668.

For each expense item, list its cost today and don't try to determine what the cost will be at retirement. Once all the amounts are determined, add them to get monthly and annual estimates of the cost of the first year of retirement. All these factors need to be considered to develop a solid estimate of the cost of the first year of retirement. It is more work than the traditional and simple methods, but the consequences of using the wrong estimate make the additional steps worthwhile. An alternative to doing the calculations by hand is to use one of the online calculators listed in Appendix B. The technology will automatically account for the irregular expenses that occur only every few years, so you won't have to factor them into your annual budget.

These website calculators will do all the computations required to complete a worksheet. In some cases, the web calculator is more streamlined than the paper version, primarily to minimize frustration for those with slower Internet connections. The best web-based retirement calculators are those from the three major no-load mutual fund firms: Vanguard, Fidelity, and T.Rowe Price. They generally have the more robust features. Here are five excellent calculators to select from that will get you started:

www.quicken.com/retirment/planner
www.smartmoney.com/retirement
www.mpower.com
www.financialengines.com
www.morningstar.com

If the results that you get from a calculator are significantly higher or lower than what you expected, don't get discouraged. The problem may be due to an unrealistic assumption. In any event, if the calculator points out a problem you may have with your retirement plan, then take action to resolve if as best as you can. The purpose of using the calculator is to help you determine what you can do today to make your retirement years more secure. The results from whatever calculator you use are only estimates.

You need to determine what your life expectancy will be so that the calculator can determine if your 401(k) and IRA money will last as long as you will. People are living longer so you might want to assume a life expectancy of 95 or 100 to help reduce your chances that you'll outlive your money. These basic assumptions will help you estimate how much money you'll need when you retire and whether you are on track to realize your goal based on the investment risk you're willing to take.

What's Your Risk Level?

Different risks levels are associated with each investment options and your tolerance for risk typically goes down as you get older. What is your investment risk tolerance? Each person has a different propensity for risk. When investing, your propensity for risk can be used to determine the percentage of your portfolio that is exposed to high or low risk equities. Find out how you feel about risk by completing the Risk Tolerance Questionnaire that follows to help determine your risk profile. If you prefer, you can take an online risk-tolerance questionnaire at www.Calc.XML. Check the results against how you've allocated your assets to make sure they line up with the risk level you are comfortable with. If you find a discrepancy, don't be in a rush to immediately change it. Remember, time is on your side so think about your options before you act.

Risk Tolerance Questionnaire

What is your age?
A) 55 or above
B) 36-54
C) 35 years or under

What do you expect to be your next major expenditure?
A) Providing for retirement
C) Buying a house
D) Paying for my kids' college education

When do you expect to use most of the money you are now accumulating in your investments?
A) At any time now...so a high level of liquidity is important
B) Probably in the future... 6-10 years from now
C) Probably in 11-20 or more years from now

Over the next several years, you expect your annual income to:
A) Stay about the same
B) Grow moderately
C) Grow substantially

Due to a general market correction, one of your investments loses 14% of its value a short time after you buy it. What do you do?
A) Sell the investment so you will not have to worry if it continues to decline
B) Hold on to it and wait for it to climb back up

C) Buy more of the same investment...because at the current lower price, it looks even better than when you bought it

Which of these investing plans would you choose for your investment dollars?

A) You would go for maximum diversity, dividing your portfolio among all available investments, including those ranging from highest return/greatest risk to lowest return/lowest risk

B) You are concerned about too much diversification, so you would divide your portfolio among two investments with historically high rates of return and moderate risk

C) You would put your investment dollars in the investment with the highest rate of return and most risk

Assuming you are investing in a stock mutual fund, which one do you choose?

A) A fund devoted to highly diversified 'blue chip' stocks that pay dividends

B) A fund that only invests in established, well-known companies that have a potential for continued growth

C) A fund of companies that may make significant technological advances that are still selling at their low initial offering price

Assuming you are investing in only one bond, which bond do you choose?

A) A tax-free bond, since minimizing taxes is your primary investment objective

B) The bond of a well-established company that pays a rate of interest somewhere between the other two bonds

C) A high-yield (junk) bond that pays a higher interest rate than the other two bonds, but also gives you the least sense of security with regard to a possible default

You expect inflation to return and it has been suggested that you invest in hard assets such as real estate, which has historically outpaced inflation. Your currently invested are long-term bonds. What do you do?

A) Ignore the advice and hold on to the bonds

B) Sell the bonds, putting half the proceeds in 'hard' assets and the other half in money market funds
C) Sell the bonds, put the proceeds in 'hard' assets, and borrow additional money so you can buy even more hard assets.

If you have answered all of the questions in the questionnaire, you are now ready to determine what your estimated risk level is. Start by counting all of your A, B, and C responses. An A responses are one point each, Bs responses are worth two points each, Cs responses are worth three points each. Multiply you number of response for each letter by its point designation, and total your score. For example, if you had 2 A responses, 5 B responses, and 2 C responses, your total score would be; 2As X 1+ 5Bs X 2 + 2Cs X 3 = 18. The range of possible scores is from a low of 9 to a high of 45. Here are the risk levels that are assigned to the different scores:

Conservative Investor Risk Level (9 to 14 Total Score)
Moderate Investor Risk Level (15 to 20 Total Score)
Aggressive Investor Risk Level (21 to 27 Total Score)

The table that follows shows the risk levels that are generally associated with the six investment categories. It will give you an idea of what risk is associated with each option. How do your current investments match up with your tolerance for risk? If they're right on, great! If there's a discrepancy, do not be too concerned about it. We'll show you how to use diversity to even out your investment to a risk level that you're comfortable with.

Investment Category Risk Assessment		
Category	Risk Level	Objectives
Cash in interest bearing accounts and government bonds	Low	Earn short-term interest rates from secure investments
Domestic Stock Funds	Medium to High	Speculates on low interest rates to get higher returns at maturity
Foreign Stock Funds	Medium to High	Follow higher average market returns
Bond Funds	Low to Medium	Looks for stocks, bonds, and commodities with reliable performance over time
Index Funds	Low to Medium	Invest in a market mix of equities, bond, and commodities
Individual Stocks	Medium to High	To obtain high rates of returns for shareholders

Rate of Return and Risk

There is no reason for retirees and pre-retirees to earn low investment rates of returns. Developing an investment plan before making any investments is a key to your success. Most investors suffer either because they don't have investment plans or they follow plans based on bad advice. They must develop an investment strategy and know when to follow it and when the strategy should be changed or they risk losing money or earning subpar returns. Learn how to allocate your portfolio among stocks, bonds, and other assets in order to achieve the right mix of investment at an acceptable rate of return at a risk level that you're comfortable with.

A conservative low-risk investor normally invests for income. In the early 1980s, a conservative investment in money market funds could earn 12 percent or more annually. Safe U.S. Treasury bonds also carried double-digit yields. But the yields on income investments declined significantly during the next 20 years. In 2010, most money market funds carried yields of 1 percent or less. Treasury bonds paid an interest rate of 3 to 5 percent. That's a big drop in income.

Stock market investors also are likely to face lower returns in the future. Stocks earned historically high returns from 1982 through 2005. The returns far exceeded the rate of growth in corporate profits. That's because the economy shifted from a period of high inflation, high interest rates, and creased benefits from these programs and should plan on the possibility of reduced benefits. Already, the average retirement age is scheduled to rise over the years. Future retirees must save more in order to offset the anticipated reduced benefits.

The reason for the nicer return was because of the greater risk an investor is willing to take. We're not advocating loading up your investment portfolio with stock funds, because that would be too risky. You don't need a high-risk portfolio to generate worthwhile returns, but you do need to think about how much risk you're comfortable with to meet your retirement goals. There are several ways to control and limit your exposure to risk on high-return investments. There are several free online financial planning tools that are available to you such as Ameritrade's Wealth Ruler (www.tdameritrade.com), Fidelity's My Plan (www.fidelity.com/myplan), and T. Rowe Price's income calculator (www.troweprice.com/ric).

Consolidating Accounts

Some boomers like to open several IRA accounts; one for mutual funds, one for stocks, one for CDs and so on, which can get confusing. Most brokerage firms like Fidelity Investments and Charles Schwab can consolidate your separate investments into one IRA account to simplify the task of managing your investments.

There are several reasons why you might want to convert your 401(k) into an IRA. An IRA can be a great substitute if your 401(k) investment lineup is performing badly. And, if your employer is not contributing to your plan, switching may be a no-brainer. You're stuck with whatever investment options your employer has deemed are best for you in a 401(k) plan. With an IRA, you're free to choose the investment options that you know are best for you. An IRA has the same tax advantages as a 401(k) in that as long as your money stays in the account, there's no need to worry about taxes.

If you invest in a Roth IRA, you don't have to worry about whether taxes will skyrocket because you won't owe taxes on the money when it's withdrawn. IRAs offer generous deadlines to make your contributions. The IRS gives you 15½ months to invest in an IRA. For example, the 2010 tax year contribution window extends from January 1, 2009 until April 15, 2010. IRAs promote disciplined savings. You can instruct the financial institution that holds your account to automatically withdraw a specified amount of money on a certain date every month from your checking or savings account. Autopilot savings is an excellent way to grow wealthy.

Diversifying Your Investments

Diversification is the process investors goes through to determine what portion of their total investment dollars should be allocated to the investment options that are available to them. The goal of diversification is to end up owning a profitable portfolio that will continue to grow in the future to meet your expected returns at a risk you're willing to take.

When you diversify the assets in your portfolio, you lessen the chance of being subjected to the volatility of the market. Your aim is to gather assets that have absolutely nothing in common so that one class of assets will cushion the blow of another class of assets when the market becomes turbulent. In times of financial turbulence, it's highly unlikely that every investment category will behave in the same way. For instance, if stock funds take a nose dive, chances are that bond funds or another category of assets in your portfolio will remain stable.

Diversifying is a way of protecting your portfolio. There are countless investment categories that you can use to make that happen. One of the best ways to reduce your risk of loss whether you invest in invest in stock funds, bond funds, or other investments, is to spread your money around so that if one investment does badly, the others may do well and make up for the loss. When you are ready to start diversifying your assets into categories, you can get as simple or as complicated as you like. If you're interested in keeping it simple, then invest in just three mutual funds that invest in domestic stocks, foreign stocks, and bonds.

Choosing Investment Options

Determining what's the right investment option for you is an important part of the investment process. Although it will require some time to set up at the outset, when you're done, you will have learned how it's done and it will be relatively easy to maintain on a periodic basis. Your first step will be to figure out how big or small each piece of your pie will be in different investment categories.

A moderate investor would be somewhere in between. They may decide to ease back on stocks to accommodate a greater weight in bonds and fixed income funds. They're willing to sacrifice some potential returns to reduce their exposure to risk. They may choose to stick to index funds to keep from getting caught up in the market's momentum.

When circumstances that are specific to you occur, you may want to change your allocation. What if your employer has run into financial problems and you fear losing your job? What if your spouse is coping with a medical emergency? If you're dealing with these kinds of situations, it's more important to become conservative and preserve your principle. Or the reverse could happen. What if you just landed the job of your dreams with a huge jump in salary? What if the stock market is doing great? Maybe you can afford to be more aggressing and enjoy a higher rate of return. Those are the kind of event that will guide you to manage your investments through good and bad times using asset allocation.

Every investment plan should include low-cost index funds or ETFs and target retirement funds. If these options available to you, your 401(k) and IRA will perform far better than most professionally managed funds over the long term. Search for funds that behave most like index funds. The right mix of investment ensures that you're being aggressive enough to earn a decent return without subjecting them to a level of volatility that may be discomforting to you.

As we have discussed, diversification of your investments is crucial to your financial success. And to keep your balance, you have got to be willing to rebalance. For example, let's say you have a 75/25 percent stock-to-bond allocation. After six months, you discover that the value of stocks are starting to fall dramatically, while bonds are appreciating nicely. It may be time to shift some of your money out of stocks and into bond. Or the reverse may be happening. The stock market is wildly bullish and bonds are flat. It might be time to take some of your winnings out of stock and store it in a money market fund until the market settles down. Selling your winners is a prudent way to keep your portfolio in good shape. You just have to have the discipline to do it. When you rebalance, don't be tempted to put everything into the winning asset. As Galileo said when he discovered gravity: "Whatever goes up must come down." That same scientific principal is also true of the investment market.

As retirement approaches, your portfolio should be shifted from riskier investments such as stocks into safer, income producing investments such as annuities, bonds, certificates of deposit, and money market funds. The theory behind this advice is simply a retiree needs regular income to pay living expenses and does not want the principal of their portfolio to fluctuate as much as stocks do. They typically want a portfolio that pays income and maintains a reasonably stable value.

Getting Investment Advice

Once you've determined how much you will need when you retire, you may want to get some advice on what steps you should take to achieve that financial goal. You need to find a person you feel comfortable with and that has the knowledge to provide you with meaningful advice. It may be a knowledgeable friend or it could be a professional advisor. Advisors often offer complimentary get-acquainted sessions. The National Association of Personal Financial Advisors (NAPFA) offers a questionnaire on their website at www.napfa.com that will help you ask the right questions when you interview candidates. Financial Planners Association at www.fplanet.org will provide you with a list of financial planners in your area.

When you begin making your initial screening calls for an advisor, let them know as specifically as you can what you need them for and ask them what services they offer. Listen carefully to their answers and take notes to help you determine if they have the expertise you need. Ask them for the names of at least three of their clients who you can contact for references. Ask your advisor candidates how they are paid.

Not everybody can afford or wants to hire a financial advisor. You may be entitled to free or inexpensive advice from the firm that administers your 401(k) and IRA. Companies like Fidelity Investments, Vanguard, T. Rowe Price, and Charles Schwab offer excellent financial advice and assistance to their clients. Their advisors can often answer common questions regarding your investment and savings goals, asset allocation, and withdrawing money from your account. All of these firms maintain outstanding websites that are crammed with great financial information and tools.

Putting It All Together

Recent surveys show that after the bear market of 2009, many people postponed their retirement. That's because it's more difficult to make retirement plans or setting a retirement date without estimating the cost of retirement and how long your financial assets are likely to last. Unfortunately, this is an area in which retirees receive poor advice or unfortunately, no advice. Most of the advice on how much to save for retirement is nothing more than very simple rules of thumb simply because we don't have much experience with extended retirements.

Longer retirements and greater self-reliance mean that you must dispense with rules of thumb and devise a more accurate estimate of retirement spending and capital needs. Ask retirees what their biggest retirement planning mistake was, and a high percentage will say that they didn't do a good enough job of estimating their retirement spending.

Ask financial professionals, and they'll say that most people don't have a good handle on how much the retirement they desire will cost. People who estimate their expenses when they retire, even if they make poor estimates, save more and are better prepared for retirement than those who do not make estimates.

Pay extra attention to your risk tolerance as you get ready to retire early. Measure your risk tolerance at least once a quarter to help you determine how changes in the economy might be affecting you and the way you've allocated your investments. If your portfolio is too volatile, you may be tempted to change your mix of assets, which could reduce the long-term value of retirement accounts. Your age needs to be a bigger factor than your risk tolerance when you retire early.

Chapter 3

Investing In Stocks

A stock can be your best friend but they can also become your worst nightmare

Companies issue stock to the public to raise funds for any number of activities. When you buy shares of stock, you're in effect buying your own slice of company ownership. You can buy stock for a variety of reasons, but it boils down to a conviction that you have faith in the company, you believe it is going to perform well in the future, and, as a result, you expect the value of the stock to increase as the company prospers.

Investing in stocks is a good option for many people mapping out a retirement investment program. They're easy to buy, offer a variety of choices, and can be used to diversify your investments. If you prefer a more hands-on approach, one where we're calling the shots instead of some fund manager, then investing in stocks may be the way to go. In this chapter, we'll introduce you to the universe of stocks. We'll examine features, pluses, drawbacks, and strategies as to how they can fit into your overall 401(k) or IRA funding strategy.

Stock Market Basics

There are three primary stock exchanges in the United States. These are where investors of all sorts come together to buy and sell stock-sometimes selling for profit, occasionally at a loss, but always with an eye for profit potential. The best known is the New York Stock Exchange. This is the largest market in terms of dollar trading activity and the second largest in terms of the number of companies it lists (roughly 3,000). Its list of companies reads as something of a who's who of the American business community.

By contrast, the American Stock Exchange is smaller-listing only about 800 companies and the companies included are generally too small to qualify for listing on the New York exchange.

The third market is the largest. The NASDAQ (National Association of Securities Dealers Automated Quotations system) takes in more than 4,000 companies. It is a purely electronic trading network and it is the busiest of the three in terms of the number of shares traded daily.

Stocks come in two basic forms. The first is referred to as common stock. This is the type of stock that the public generally buys. The second form is common stock, which represents a share of ownership in the company and also makes you eligible for any dividends the company may generate. Additionally, should the company fail financially, common stock entitles you to some form of payback-albeit often a small one-after creditors and others to whom the company owes money have been paid off.

Preferred stock has more financial muscle than common stock. For one thing, dividends are guaranteed and they're often larger than common stock dividends. And, should the company collapse, preferred stock holders are ahead of common stock owners when it comes to getting what proceeds remain. Common categories of stock include:

Growth stocks are issued by companies that are growing both in operations and in income. The price of the stock usually follows suit. Since growth stocks tend to reinvest much of what they earn, it's rare that growth stocks pay dividends to investors. They can be among the riskiest of stocks to buy. If all goes well and the company flourishes, you can be in on the payoff. If the company falters-or even if the industry in which the company operates takes a hit-growth stocks can take a beating, often never to recover.

Value stocks are similar to growth stocks in that investors expect them to go up in value. The difference here is that the price of value stocks is out of whack investors have yet to recognize their real value and, as a result, value stocks are undervalued and available at a discount. Like growth stocks, however, if the company doesn't shine as expected, that depressed stock price may stay right where it is.

Income stocks are designed to produce reliable income through high dividends. These tend to be large, very well established companies and are usually far more predictable than growth or value stocks.

Blue chip stocks include some of the biggest, most recognizable companies around, including IBM, Coca-Cola, and others. These pay substantial, reliable dividends and can offer some growth as well. The downside is they can be among the most expensive stocks to buy.

International stocks are issued by companies outside the United States. In fact, under the umbrella of international, they can take in all sorts of other stocks, including growth, value, and income. International stocks can often serve as a complement to domestic stocks, as they often don't react in step with the American markets.

Separating Winners from Losers

Choosing the right stock, or mix of stocks for your portfolio can be a challenge, particularly for something as important as your retirement. Many people devote their entire lives to this field of study. We'll start with some basic ideas and strategies to get you started. For all the complexity in choosing winning stocks, there are some overriding basics that need to be taken into consideration.

Look at the company's annual report as an essential first step in getting to know a company's stock. An annual report offers a detailed view of a company's varied makeup and activities, including precisely what the company does, its management, its history, types of revenue, and other critical information. Without this basic knowledge, all the subsequent analysis in the world may be useless.

Look at long-term trends to see which way the company is headed. Are its sales and income increasing? Are they expanding into new markets? And, just as important, are they doing all the right things with a reliable degree of consistency? Compare it with similar companies. Again, as with mutual funds, a stock in a vacuum may appear as rosy as can be. That glowing picture can blur if you discover that others in the same business are doing far better. When getting to know a company, compare it with its competitors and others in its field. Match up sales, profits, and overall growth to see if those numbers shine when compared with others trying to achieve the same sort of objectives.

A company's annual report is, on the whole, framed to put the company in the best light possible. After all, it goes to investors-existing and prospective so its job one to keep them happy and confident. But there's one part of the annual report where that spin isn't quite so viable. The income statement and balance sheet are about as empirical a look as you'll get at a company-the numbers, statistics, and other data that can reveal a variety of information about a company's current status as well as its prospects. That means it's important that you know what to look for in conducting your fundamental analysis. Major components of an income and balance sheet are summarized as follows:

Current assets are the amount of assets that the company has on hand that can be turned into cash within the space of one year.

Current liabilities are debt that the company has to meet within one year. Compare this with assets to make sure the company has sufficient funds at the ready to meet its short-term obligations.

Total liabilities and equity represents every part of the company that is effectively owned by someone else. This has to match up with total assets.

Total revenue is the overall amount of sales before taxes are deducted.

Cost of sales is how much all that wonderful revenue is costing the company. If this exceeds revenues, that's a major red flag-sales are coming with too heavy a price tag.

Pretax income is how much the company earns prior to the bite of taxes. It's not unheard of for some companies to earn a profit, only to shell out more in taxes.

Net income is the amount of money a company earns after taxes-as reliable a bellwether of a company's strength as you can find.

Earnings per share (EPS) show the amount of earnings per share of company stock-another critical statistic.

Technical Performance

Many investors attempt to buy a stock at a low point and sell it later for a profit when it rises. And that, in turn, can best be determined by watching how a stock trades. This is referred to as *technical analysis*. It actually breaks down into two salient price and volume. As far as price is concerned, analysts look at long-term trading patterns. They're interested in price points that historically mark a low point in a stock's value and a high point that a stock often encounters difficulty moving past often referred to as its resistance level. They'll use this information to make stock buy and sell decisions (see graph below).

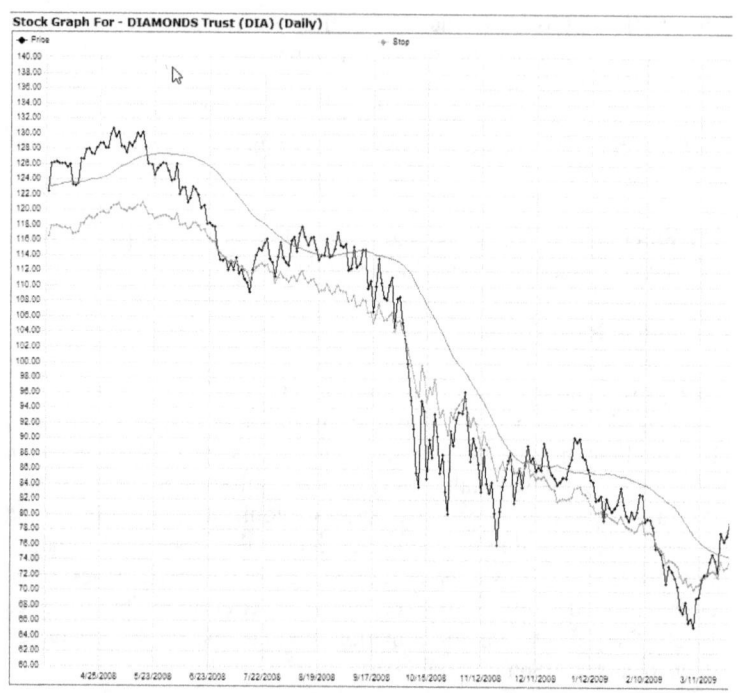

Dow Jones Industrial Average (DIA)
March 2008 – March 2009

Using these patterns, analysts try to predict at which point a stock has hit a low and, by the same token, when it appears to have topped off. Additionally, they study volume, or the amount of trading that occurs in a particular stock. This, they say, is indicative of investor interest in a stock-yet another factor that can push its value up or down. Stockchart.com is an online site that allows you to create charts of any stock, index or mutual fund that are in their data base, free (see the Stockchart.com figure that follows).

Search the Site:

Search

Tools
Market Summary
Gallery View
SharpCharts
Market Carpet
PerfCharts
P&F Charts
Stock Scans
Data Adjustments

Charts
Your Favorite Charts
Public Chart Lists
CandleGlance Groups
Breadth Charts
Dynamic Yield Curve
Historical Charts
SharpCharts Voyeur
Ticker Cloud | Ticker Rain

Join Now!
◀◀◀ Join Now for ▶▶▶
Personalized Charts!

Information
About Us
Free Newsletter
Business Products
Privacy Statement

Our Bookstore
Monthly Specials
ChartWatchers' Bundle
Tech. Analysis Books
John Murphy's Books
P&F Charting Books

Stockcharts.com Free Charts

The following tools are designed to give you a taste of our charting services

SharpCharts

Our most popular charts! Create bar, candlestick or line charts for any stock, index or mutual fund in our database.

Create a chart: [ ] [Go!]

Point & Figure Charts

An old-school classic with a high-tech twist. Point & Figure charts reduce visual noise by filtering out less significant price moves.

Create a chart: [ ] [Go!]

Performance Charts

Our interactive "PerfCharts" let you compare the performance of any set of securities over various periods of time.

Use this tool now ▶

Market Carpets

A StockCharts.com exclusive! Scan large collections of stocks quickly to spot various signals in this unique graphical display.

Use this tool now ▶

Additional Tools

Predefined Scan Results

Find stocks that fit a pattern or have reached new highs or lows.

Use this tool now ▶

Market Summary

Get the pulse on the market! Major market averages, sector and industry indices and more.

Use this tool now ▶

Stock Ratios

Numbers and statistics can offer great insight into a company's operations and its prospects for success. The downside is there can be an awful lot of numbers, not to mention the challenges of piecing them all together to form a coherent picture. Fortunately, there are a number of stock analysis calculations that do that very thing for investors. Known as ratios, you'll often see these cited by investment analysts and other financial professionals as they discuss stock selection. That may suggest complicated mathematics, but it's really not so complicated as all that. Here are several ratios, how they work, and what they can tell you about a particular stock.

The price/earnings ratio (P/E) is perhaps the most popular ratio used to analyze stock. In its essence, it illustrates how much an investor would be willing to spend in return for $1 in company earnings. In that respect, the formula involves dividing the stock price by the earnings per share. The telling point of a P/E ratio can indicate

47

several things. For instance, a high P/E means that investors are willing to pay more for a stock than its current earnings might warrant. That can be a sign of a company that's expected to do great things. One example of a high P/E was Google, which topped 100 a few years back (the average P/E range is 15 to 25 or so).

But a high P/E can also be a sign of risk. If nothing else, the price of the company's stock is out of whack with what it is earning. That can suggest a stock that the market has simply valued inappropriately. Book value reflects the real value of a company. It's calculated by totaling all assets and subtracting debt and liabilities. One way to use a P/E is to compare a particular company with others in its industry. That way, you can see if the industry as a whole is fairly valued or if, by chance, one company's value has yet to be noticed by investors.

The price/book ratio or P/B compares a company's stock price against its net worth. It's calculated by dividing current stock price by a firm's *book value*. The ratio compares a stock's price to what a company is worth, rather than what it may be earning at a particular time. In that sense, the lower the P/B, the greater the chance of a good buy, as that indicates investors as a group have yet to recognize the genuine worth of a company. A ratio of 1 or less is considered low. The average P/B for Standard and Poor's 500 stocks is a bit less than 3. Many investors prefer price/book value to other ratios. Their thinking is that a company's value is hard to disguise or somehow make more appealing, which is always possible with earnings.

The price/sales ratio S/P involves the price of a company stock alongside sales figures. This is calculated by dividing a current stock price by a company's earnings per share. Like other ratios, the lower the S/P, the greater the possibility that a company has plenty of upside potential. The average S/P ratio for the Standard and Poor's 500 is 2.3. By contrast, a high ratio can top 16, while a low ratio can be below 1.

The best way to use ratios is to take advantage of every element that each ratio offers. If possible, employ more than one in breaking down a company's financials. That way, you stand the best chance of getting the more comprehensive and telling financial picture you can of a stock.

Risk-Reward Relationships

You need to choose reasonable stocks that fit into your financial goals for retirement and satisfy your tolerance for risk. Two investments with different levels of risk can produce very different rewards. For example, the following figure illustrates how much of a favorable impact an additional 3 percent return will have on your portfolio.

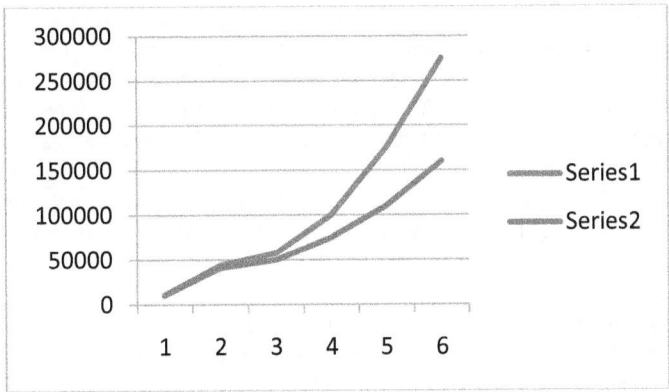

Our example compares two hypothetical investments in stocks that share the different risk levels. The one with the higher risk has a 3 percent higher annual return than the one with a lower risk - 9 versus 6 percent. But, look at the huge difference in the end balance of $275,000 for the 9 percent return versus $160,000 for the 6 percent return over 30 years. The 3 percent higher return would have generated a 75 percent higher return of dollars ($115,000) to your retirement accounts.

When it comes to investing, the amount of risk you can tolerate has nothing to do with what you like to do like sky diving or drive fast cars. It has more to do with your time horizon to retire and the

49

amount of time you're willing to expend monitoring your investments. Can you handle a 10 percent, 25 percent, or even a bigger drop in the value of your 401(k)? Your answer to questions like these will help you determine whether to invest in risky stock funds or safer bond funds. Imagine yourself with $100,000 in your 401(k) that drops to $50,000 in value. Would you be able to hang on or, in anguish, put the money you have left over in lower-risk investments? If you sell your high-risk bond fund, you'll have to dramatically increase your contribution to make up for both the loss and the lower investment return you will get in the bond fund.

Many investors are comfortable owning high-risk stock funds when the market is doing well but tend to sell when the market takes a nosedive. But they know how to manage their risk level. Let's repeat the scenario where you had invested $100,000 in a high-risk stock fund. You had determined that you were comfortable with accepting a 10 percent risk level and were willing to actively monitor the investment in your portfolio. When the stock market starts to take a nose dive, you do what every investor has a right to do: you sell your stocks and buy a lower rick investment, thereby limiting your loss to just $1,000 (based on the $100,000 investment example).

The whole point of finding a comfortable risk level is that it helps you stick to your retirement plan. Investing and managing high-risk investments give you an opportunity to enjoy higher returns if you are willing to take the time to monitor both the upsides and downsides of the market. If you're not willing to do this, then choose a good, solid low-risk investment that typically generates a lower return. If you invest too conservatively, your money may not grow enough to offset inflation. Even though you're earning some return, prices may be rising faster because of inflation, leaving you with less spending power when you retire. If you invest too aggressively, the ups and downs may be more than you can stand.

Tracking Your Stocks

Knowing how your stocks are doing at any moment in time is critical to the overall management of your plan. That's called tracking your investments in a portfolio to see if they're reaching the eventual results you're looking for, in your time frame for an important reasons; you can better predict what the future performance portfolio may be by knowing how they have been performing. It ensures that you own a variety of investment categories to reduce risk while maintaining or increasing your expected returns. Fortunately, there are a number of portfolio investment tracking tools that are available to you online that are listed in the online appendix of the book. The following example illustrates how a portfolio tracking tool can be used to tell you how your investments are doing:

Portfolio Summary for VVTop10 as of - 7/30/2009

Investment	$100,000.00
Equity	$36,210.00
Buying Power	$169,171.90
Interest	$0.00
Net	$2,690.95
Cash	$66,480.95
Total Value	$102,690.95
Margin	$0.00
Gain/Loss %	2.69%

Company	Symbol	Purchase Date	Type	Cost / Share	Last	Gain / Share	REC	Quantity	Cost Basis	Market Value	Gain
ClickSoftware	CKSW	7/17/2009	Long	$7.76	$7.78	$0.02		1000	$7,759.95	$7,780.00	$20.05
Kirkland's Inc	KIRK	7/17/2009	Long	$13.76	$13.54	-$0.22		1000	$13,759.95	$13,540.00	-$219.95
Medifast Inc	MED	7/17/2009	Long	$14.36	$14.89	$0.53		1000	$14,359.95	$14,890.00	$530.05

Stock Buying and Selling Strategies

Buying stock is simple; you choose one that looks good and hope it goes up in value. But there are several strategies that augment that basic function to better your chances for success. Here are four that may prove particularly helpful.

Dollar-cost averaging is where you invest a set amount of money on a regular basis, regardless of whether the stock is going up or down. The thinking is if the stock has gone down in price, you're able to buy more shares. And, if the stock has gone up in price-who's complaining? This can help you amass a greater holding for your retirement in a cost-effective manner. But note: because of commissions, dollar-cost averaging is more suitable for mutual funds than individual stocks.

Value averaging is a variant on dollar-cost averaging that takes into account stock price movement. For instance, say you wish to invest $300 every month. If, by the end of that first month, the stock has gone down to $280 in value, you next invest $320 to bring the overall amount for the two months up to $600 as planned. By the same token, if the stock goes up to $330, you only have to invest $270 to reach the $600 target level.

Limit orders is a system that lets you establish prices at which you wish to buy or sell. Here,
you specify where you want to get involved with a stock say one you like is at $45 and you want to buy at $40. You then instruct your broker (or the online system) to buy it when it drops to that level. If it goes lower, the sell order kicks in at the lower price. The same procedure works for selling. If you order a sale at $50, that's when the sale occurs. If the price goes higher, you automatically sell at the higher price. This helps lock in gains for your retirement.

Stop loss Orders is specifically designed to limit your losses and protect whatever profit you may have earned from a stock. To illustrate: you buy a stock at $10 and it moves to $30. You then set up a stop loss at $20-ifthe stock moves to that level, the stock is automatically sold protecting a $10 per share profit. Don't set up a stop loss too close to a stock's current price-say, $28 on a stock currently valued at $30. You may protect your profit, but you may also be selling yourself short if the drop is only a short-term bump after which the stock soars.

Using Brokers

There is any number of ways to buy stock to fund your retirement. Here's a rundown of the choices available to you, along with their varied advantages and drawbacks. For years, this was the sole option for anyone interested in buying stocks. The methodology is simple. You open an account at a brokerage house and you start working with a broker. From there, you buy stocks and craft a portfolio, just as you would with any other means of buying stocks.

The difference is in service and the expense you pay for that service. A broker charges a commission every time he or she executes a trade on your behalf. While that varies from one brokerage house to the next, the cost can often be substantial. Going with a full-service broker has its advantages and drawbacks. There are investors who swear by their broker, citing their guidance and oversight. Others value the resources that many full-service brokers can provide, from research to programs designed to better educate investors. However, the cost per trade can be substantial.

In return for that expense, a good broker should work closely with you to develop a portfolio that's suited to your needs. Not only should this involve a fair amount of interaction between the two of you so your broker gets to know you, your investment style, and your needs, a solid broker should also be proactive. That means he or she will call with ideas that they think jibe with your situation. To illustrate: one discount firm chosen at random charges $17.95 for a phone trade involving up to 1000 shares. On average, discounters charge anywhere from one third to one tenth what full service fees might levy in commission.

The tradeoff is there's a good deal less hand-holding with discounters. For the most part, it's up to you to do the research behind your investment decisions and many discounters have substantial online research tools. These are the cheapest of the cheap. Another example chosen at random: one online firm charges a flat $10 for all Internet-based trades, no matter the number of shares involved. Again, like other houses, the fee jumps substantially once you stray off the Internet, $35 over the phone and $75 or more if you meet with a broker.

What does it take to enter your own trade online instead of using a broker? The simple answer that is illustrated in the following figure is about a minute of your time on the Internet. You basically enter the stock's trade abbreviation like IBM and the dollar amount that you want to invest in the fund, and press the enter key.

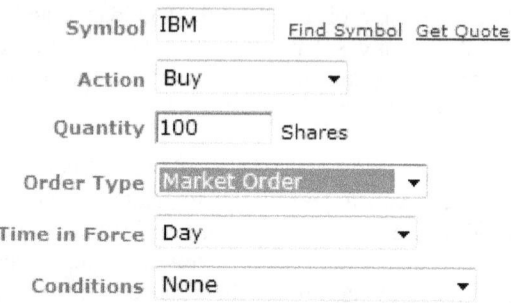

Online Order Screen

Recently, the line between full-service and discount firms has blurred. Full-service brokers now offer less-expensive Internet-based services, while discounters are providing more traditional services. So why are investors willing to pay large brokers' fees for questionable returns? Individual investors often assume that brokers know more about what they're doing than they do. In most of their dealings with their clients, brokers aren't considered fiduciaries. A fiduciary is ethically bound to put their client's interest first as opposed to their own interest.

The fees that you pay when you buy individual stocks or funds online are typically 10 percent or less that what you'd pay a broker to do. Of course, when you order online, you presumably have done all of the appropriate research on your investment choice before you entered the order.

Putting It All Together

As a general rule, the more risk you're willing to take, the more return you'll realize. Choose reasonable investments that fit into your financial goals for retirement and satisfy your tolerance for risk. If you are working with a broker, make sure he or she is living up to your expectations. Just remember, the fees that you pay when you buy individual stocks or funds online are typically 10 percent or less that what you'll pay a broker to do.

If you have a 401(k) plan that allows you to invest in stocks, they can provide great long-term growth potential. But, like other investments, be sure to diversify. When choosing a stock, use the company's annual report to get to know the company inside and out. Know how profitable it is and how much debt it carries. Investigate various types of brokerage operations carefully. Don't necessarily sacrifice service for cost. Strategies such as dollar-cost averaging and stop loss orders can also be effective tools in developing a winning stock portfolio.

If you are working with a broker, make sure he or she is living up to your expectations. If they try to and succeed in putting you into trendy investments that tank, find another broker. Good ones will help you build long-term investment plans that are in concert with your tolerance for risk. Be wary of the broker who always wants you to invest in a fund that his firm has picked. If they have a "preferred" list, make sure they can explain to your satisfaction, why each investment is preferred and what are the risks involved.

Chapter 4

Investing in Mutual Funds

Good funds are easy to find if you know where to look for them

The first mutual fund, known as the Massachusetts Investors Trust, was set up in 1924. Choosing the mutual funds for your retirement plan isn't necessarily simple nor should it be taken lightly. The benefits of selecting just the right fund can have far-reaching positive effects on your 401(k) and IRA plans. In this chapter, we'll introduce you to what, for many boomers, is the bedrock of their retirement plan - mutual funds. We'll also offer some ideas and strategies to help you find just the right funds for your retirement plan.

Mutual Fund Basics

An investment company that pools money from many investors and, in turn, invests it in a broad array of stocks, bonds, and other types of securities creates a mutual fund(s) in the process. The workings of a mutual fund are simple in their essence. When you buy shares in a fund, you are joining other investors who have also bought into the fund. A professional fund manager then handles those funds, buying and selling various investments in hopes of producing the best performance possible for the overall portfolio that's in their fund. The thousands of mutual funds currently available to investors offer a wide variety of advantages, including:

Diversification. This may be as significant a plus as mutual funds may offer any sort of investor. Investing on our own with the often limited funds available to us makes sufficient diversification difficult. By their very function, through the pooling of your investment dollars alongside those of other investors, mutual funds can offer virtually instant diversification across a wide variety of investments, including stocks, bonds, and cash.

Lower investment risk. By spreading holdings over a number of investments-some aggressive, others more conservative-investment risk can be reduced. And mutual funds provide that very type of diversification.

Professional management. Few of us are genuinely adept at picking winning investments-at least, on a consistent basis. When you invest in a mutual fund, your money is being overseen by a team of financial professionals. Moreover, they're on the job all the time. Unless you have free time to constantly monitor an investment portfolio, that's a level of attention that's hard to match.

Expense management. Buying and selling stocks on a regular basis can add up in commission costs, even if you use a discount broker. By comparison, many mutual funds operate very efficiently, resulting in reasonable costs for investors.

Since there are so many funds from which to choose, it's not difficult to find one to match any sort of investment style or goal. Investing in a mutual fund requires doing your homework and then giving the money to someone else to handle. If you're a hands-on sort of person, that lack of involvement may be unnerving. Some funds invest in companies that you might not wish to support.

Types of Funds

With an overview of mutual funds' basic performance features and other information as to how they work, we can start becoming acquainted with the various types of available funds. We'll cover each fund's major features and the advantages and drawbacks to each to help you find a suitable fund to invest in for retirement.

Aggressive growth funds take a forceful approach by investing in companies that, while they may be relatively small now, have the greatest potential for success-and, hence, appreciation of stock value. These are suited to people with a long-term investment horizon-say, someone in their 20s and 30s who have a sufficiently long time frame and can ride out market volatility. On the other hand, these are not suited for people nearing retirement, as they may not have enough time to rebound from unexpected drops in the market.

Growth funds are similar to aggressive growth funds, but are a bit more toned down. They're a blend of growth companies, so they're aggressive. On the other hand, they try to balance that with more conservative holdings, such as large companies whose stocks yield high dividends. They also look for companies whose stock has real potential for growth, but with less potential volatility. These funds are suited to investors with a shorter time frame before retirement. They're also suited to anyone interested in growth but not the ups and downs that aggressive growth funds can experience.

Index funds are sometimes referred to as sector funds. They are good options ff you'd be happy just matching the returns of a broad range of the market. They tend to buy and hold stocks rather than engage in extensive trading and selling, they can also be more cost-effective to own than more active funds. Index funds can take in companies from a broad range of industries and concentrate on specific economic sectors. These can include areas such as health care, energy, or specific forms of technology. They can be among the most aggressive funds from which to choose.

Small-cap, mid-cap, and large-cap funds tend to invest in companies ranging in value of $2 billion to $10 billion, are a bit more conservative than growth funds. Large-caps look for stability and income; as a result, they target only large, very well-established firms.

International funds as the name implies, invest in companies located outside the United States. Some look to capitalize on areas of the world just beginning to develop economically while others target countries that are more developed and stable.

Socially responsible funds are often referred to as "green" funds. These are funds that limit their portfolios to companies that have good environmental records, good labor practices, or other attributes the fund would see as socially valuable. As such, these funds don't just look at a company's performance and financials, they also want to know how the company got to where it is.

Real estate investment trusts funds (REITs) are funds that invest in property, including shopping centers, apartment buildings, and similar commercial operations.

Finding Quality Funds

Consider the risk you're willing to take before you invest in a particular fund. Don't view risk as a four-letter word because there's nothing wrong with investing in risky funds. You'll need to assume some risk to achieve healthy gains. What's important is that you understand a fund's risk and can handle both financially and emotionally against any potential loss.

The Mutual Fund 2007 tables on Money magazine's website (www.Money.com) provide insights about a fund's level of risk. Funds are assigned a volatility ranking in the table, which measures the swings in a fund's returns. Volatility is great when funds are rising in value, but volatile funds tend to suffer the most in inhospitable markets or when their managers simply make bad decisions. The volatility rankings compare like stock funds against each other.

Size up the funds that interest you. Bigger can be better, but it can also be a hindrance to good results in the future. Expenses at bigger funds are often significantly lower than those of smaller funds. That's a plus but if a fund grows too big, it can become too unwieldy to manage effectively. In particular, the mere act of buying or selling stocks in vast quantities can move their prices in an unfavorable direction.

Money Magazine offers Money 70 at their website (www.money.com) show in the figure that follows. Select the Personal Finance option at the top of the main menu, and then select Mutual Funds to get to Money 70. Using Money 70, you can narrow down hundreds of funds to just a few who offer low fees and perform well, making your choice easier. It'll display a mix of high-quality funds that rank in the top half of their peers over five years that you can use to build a diversified portfolio. When it comes to actively managed funds, it also looks for funds that have consistent strategies and superb management experience. Money's site also checks Morningstar's stewardship fund rating grades, which rates such factors as a fund group's culture and regulatory history.

Balanced funds combine equity stakes with bond components, making them a good mix for conservative investors. There are hundreds of balanced funds, but only a few make the cut when they're narrowing down the possible MONEY 70 candidates based on their fees and performance. The concept behind these funds is simple; the equity portion is usually around 60 percent of assets, which gives shareholders a way to participate in any rally without the risk of an all-stock or all-bond portfolio. Balanced offerings will typically lag all-stock funds, but when the market reverses course, the bonds help cushion the blow by producing returns that beat their competitors.

There are no firm rules about what constitutes a fund that's too big. Much depends on the kinds of stocks a fund owns. In general, be wary of a fund that invests in large companies if its assets exceed $30 billion, particularly if the fund trades a lot. Kiplinger magazine's website (www.Kiplinger.com) features more than 3,000 funds that you can review in your leisure. To make the job easier, you can see which funds are the top 25 a five-year period. They group the funds into over 30 fund categories and update them monthly so you only need to select the categories that are of interest to you. To see the fund rankings, go to www.Kiplinger.com/links/mutualfunds (See their website that follows).

Don't just pick a fund that has recently performed well. Look for funds that have performed well over the last two or three year are also rated "high" by Morningstar (www.Morningstar.com). It's one of the premiere mutual fund rating companies in the country. Funds are rated with one to five stars where a 1-star is the lowest rating and a 5-star is the highest. Avoid funds that have annual expense ratios that are greater than 1.5 percent of the fund's total assets.

In a chaotic economy, it's better to invest in financially strong funds that offer the potential for stable and dependable growth. You can determine that yourself by looking at the yield curve and rates that are being paid by short- and long-term bonds. Since longer-dated bonds typically pay more than short-term debt, the yield curve usually slopes upward.

We have all been told that stock funds are long-term investments that only fluctuate in value over the short-term. However, the erratic market gyrations that have occurred over the past couple of years don't support this scenario. If you agree, there are steps you can take to limit your loss of any stock fund you own. You have to be willing to exercise a stop-loss or will-sell price on any stock fund you buy. Here's how it works. To keep the numbers simple, let's say you bought one share of XYZ Stock Fund for $100. At the time you bought it, you had determined that the maximum loss you were willing to accept was 10 percent or a stop-loss price of $90. You also determined that wanted to make 20 percent or a will-sell price of $120.

Sometime after you bought XYZ Stock Fund, it goes up $20 or $120 a share. At this point, you're happy and sell, realizing a 20 percent gain. If the price had gone in the other direction, you would have exercised your stop-loss scenario and sold at $90 to minimize your loss to 10 percent and any further losses that might have occurred.

Investing in Stock Funds

Stock funds are made up of a diversified pool of stocks that are professionally managed. They're popular with people who are not interested in picking individual stocks for portfolios. The fund's managers do that for you either on an active or passive management basis. Actively managed funds employ managers who are constantly evaluating the market and selecting investment they believe will do better or outperform others.

Domestic stock funds can be made up of a mix of large-cap, mid-cap, and small-cap U.S. Stocks or they can be made up of one of those three categories. Foreign stocks funds typically invest in economies that are growing faster than ours, like China, India, and Brazil. Passively managed funds follow the logic that it's unlikely active fund managers will beat the market over the long term. Therefore, passively managed funds seek simply to match the performance of the market over the short and long term by buying investment that replicate a particular market's index. You pay a higher fee for actively managed stock funds than you do for passively managed funds.

Over the past 10 years, investors who bet on stock funds lost more than 20 percent of their holdings, while those who wagered on bond funds saw their money nearly double. So why buy stocks funds? If you believe the stock market will fully restore itself, then they will offer you higher returns for assuming greater risk than if you buy bond funds. Extended stretches of equity underperformance have proved to be great stock fund buying opportunities for those investors who were patient and value-minded.

Making money in the stock funds often involves making the right call about what's about to happen. No one can know the future, but what if you had a way to identify stocks that are on the way up before they attract a lot of attention? The fundamentalists, who tend to invest for the long term in stock funds, believe that undervalued stock funds are most likely to go up in price over time. They also believe that funds with consistent and solid growth rates are primarily comprise of or include low-risk stocks. Others who tend to invest for the short-term, look for evidence, such as price movement to the upside.

Both of these schools of thought have merit. Therefore, buy safe, undervalued stock funds, rising in price. Experience has shown that if you want to make money in both bull and bear markets you must let the trend be your friend. You must buy rising funds in a rising markets and sell falling funds in a falling market.
While some market timers may trade frequently, others change from buy to sell or vice versa on occasion. In any case, pulling out of the

market during its most uncertain period results in a smoother and more profitable ride for your 401(k) and IRA portfolio compared to a buy-and-hold approach. There are a number of other index funds like DIA, that track different segments of the market that you may be invested in or are thinking about investing in, so use them to help time the market. They're summarized in the table that follows:

Trade Symbol – Fund Name	What Each Fund Tracks
DSG – DOW JONES SMALLCAP GROWTH	It seeks to replicate the returns the Dow Jones Wilshire Small Cap Growth Index.
DSV – DOW JONES SMALLCAP VL	The fund primarily invests in the companies that replicate the performance of the Dow Jones Wilshire Small Cap Value Index.
IRY – S&P HEALTH CARE	The FUND seeks to replicate the Standard & Poor 500 stock index.
XLK – TECHNOLOGY	It is composed of companies involved in such industries as Internet software, information technology and computers.
XLI – INDUSTRIAL	It mainly invests in an array of industrial companies. These industries include aerospace and defense and building products.
XLE – ENERGY SELECT	It mainly invests in companies that primarily develop and produce crude oil and natural gas.
XLF – FINANCIAL SELECT	It invests in an array of financial service firms with diversified business lines ranging from commercial to investment banking.
XLU – UTILUTIES	It invests in companies that

SELECT	produce, generate, transmit or distribute electricity or natural gas.
XLV – HEALTHCARE	It invests in the companies that replicate the performance of companies listed on the S&P Health Care Select Sector Index.
KBE – KBW BANK	It invests in stocks of companies operating in the banking sector and regional banking institutions.
FEZ – DJ EURO STOCKS	The fund invests in the European equity markets of include Finland, France, Germany, Italy, Netherlands and Spain.
SPY – S&P DEP RECEIPTS	It invests in the growth stocks of large-cap companies. The fund seeks to replicate the performance of the S&P 500 Index.

Investing in Index Funds

If you're tired of paying the high expenses charged by mutual funds and burned by the industry's dismal returns, then consider investing in low-cost index funds. Index funds are a fixed market basket of stocks, bonds, and other securities that track the performance of a specific stock or bond indexes. Index funds have several advantages over traditional funds. Most trade just like a stock where a commission is charged on each buy or sell trade they're typically cheaper to own. They can be bought or sold at any time during a trading day. Traditional mutual funds can be bought or sold only once in a trading day by a broker at full brokerage commissions.

You're often required to hold a traditional mutual fund for a stipulate period of time before you can sell it. Otherwise, you'll be subject to an early sales penalty.

Index funds were created 20 years ago when the American Stock Exchange launched a series of index fund that were given the nickname of SPDR after the insect spider. SPDR Gold Shares trades under the exchange symbol GLD and tracks the price of gold whereas SPDR Large Cap (ELG) tracks the price of large cap stocks. For the next decade, they were used largely by institutions and wealthy individuals as a way to hedge the market. After the mutual fund scandal erupted in 2003, retail investors started dumping their mutual funds and replaced them with index funds.

Many mutual fund companies, irritated by the increasing popularity of index funds, have added them to their lineup regular funds. Some of them have exorbitant expense ratios so look for index funds with the lowest expense ratio. You can find them at the major fund houses like Vanguard, T. Rowe Price, Fidelity, and Charles Schwab. A number of firms, including Fidelity and Vanguard, have created target retirement funds that automatically rebalance at regular intervals. These funds have different asset allocations that depend on your target retirement date. As you get closer to your retirement age, these funds typically become more conservative in their asset balance.

Vanguard offers three index funds that illustrate what you should be looking for. Their total stock market index fund (VTSMX) contains large, medium and small companies mostly in the U.S. Their international stock fund (VGTSX) covers large, medium and small international companies. They also have a bond index fund (VBMFX) that invests in high-quality domestic bonds. For more information about Vanguard's index funds, visit their website at www.Vanguard.com. For more information on ETFs, visit www.amex.com, www.nyse.com or www.nasdaq.com. To compare funds by cost, use the Mutual Fund Expense Analyzer at www.nasd.com.

With a mind-boggling array of mutual funds to choose from, it's no wonder millions of Americans throw up their hands and surrender management of their finances to brokers, financial planners and other advisers. That's a shame because you don't have to be a rocket scientist to pick funds astutely. By investing in index funds on your own, you can save a substantial amount of money because you won't pay sales commissions to a broker or a percentage of your assets to an adviser to do something you can do yourself.

Home in on a specific category because the index fund world is a big place. It contains stock funds, bond funds, money-market funds and all kinds of hybrids, which may own stocks, bonds, Treasury bills and sometimes even commodities. And there are a myriad of choices within each broad category. Some funds, for example, invest in big companies while others invest in small or medium-size companies. Funds that invest in rapidly growing companies with high-priced stocks are different from those that care less about a company's growth prospects and more about buying its stock at a bargain price.

Investing in Target Date Index Funds

Target-date index funds invest is an asset allocation that's suitable for investors with particular retirement time frames. As their name, Target Date reflects the target date that their asset allocation represents like Retirement Plan 2020, which would have an allocation targeted toward investors retiring in 2020. As 2020 approaches, the fund's managers adjust the assets in the plan from high-risk investments like stocks to low-risk investments like Treasury bonds. If you decide to stay with the fund after you retire, the managers continue to reduce the investment risk to a more conservative portfolio. Target-date funds are popular choices in retirement plans because they take the guesswork out of picking and allocating your own investments.

You can also use target date funds tailored to match your tolerance for risk instead of your target retirement date. For example, if your target retirement date is 2015, but you would like to be more aggressive in your investments, you could use the 2020 fund. Conversely, if you want to be more conservative, you could use the 2020 fund. Some mutual fund companies offer lifestyle funds that are similar to target-date funds, but cater to your level of risk (i.e., conservative, moderate or high). Compare the funds of several companies before deciding which one(s) to invest in.

Investing in Exchange Traded Fund

Exchange Traded Funds or ETFs as they are more commonly called are passively managed funds. They are typically made up of market basket of securities (i.e., a mixture of different securities) and are traded like stocks on the market exchanges, such as the New York Stock Exchange. They offered instant diversification, representing a section of the market in a single security, and, like a stock, investors can buy or sell an ETF at any time. Gold and other metal-based ETFs are popular inflation hedges.

Basically, ETFs are mutual funds that trade like stocks. Some copy the returns of broad stock and bond market indexes. Others replicate the performance of baskets of stocks in single industries or in niche investments, such as long-term growth ETFs designed for investors with a healthy tolerance for risk like Russell 3000 (IWV).

Growth and income ETFs like LQD generally buy high-quality U.S. corporate bonds, foreign government bonds (IGOV), and junk bonds (HDY). Foreign market ETFs like EFA and DWX generally invest in countries that have faster growing economies than the U.S., which allows you to diversify your investment in different currencies. Because of their low fees, ETFs are a great way to invest in bonds (PCY and LOD) and commodities such as energy (DBE), gold (GLD), and agricultural products (DBA).

For the most safety, go with ETFs that track the major asset classes and come from a provider with a long, stable history like Vanguard. You can build a portfolio with just a few index funds that will give you plenty of diversification. They're a great way to build a portfolio that matches your investment style. For example, you can construct an aggressive portfolio made up solely of stock ETFs. Or if you prefer a balanced approach, you can mix stock and bond funds. You can also use ETFs as an inexpensive way to boost your exposure to, say, fast-growing companies or emerging markets. To learn about more about the advantages of investing in ETFs, go to www.Kinplinger.com and tap into one of their many excellent sub-menus that cover the subject.

Automatically Investing in Funds

Automatic investing in funds (i.e., monthly) is an option you may want to consider if it's available on your employer-sponsored 401(k) plan. Or, you can accumulate cash in your money market fund for investing in funds periodically. It's a good idea to compare fees and rules at each company that offers automatic fund investing. Fidelity, for instance, waives minimum investments in funds for participants in its automatic-asset-builder plan, but not all companies do.

Fidelity Investments waives minimum investments on many of its funds for automatic investors but requires transfers of at least $100. The transfers can be monthly, quarterly or on a more customized schedule. There are no fees for transfers to a Fidelity account, but investing in some non-Fidelity funds costs $5 per transaction. The usual transaction fee for buying those funds online is $75, according to the Fidelity fee schedule.

ETFs don't carry the minimum investment limits like traditional funds generally do, but brokerages often charge a transaction fee for every investment. American Century Investments allows automatic transfers and investments of as little as $50 as long as they total at least $600 a year. But the initial minimum investment for most American Century funds is $2,500. For its Live Strong and One Choice funds, targeted to an investor's expected retirement date or risk tolerance, the minimum is $500 as long as the customer transfers at least $100 a month to the account.

Fund Families

A fund family is a company that maintains several different mutual funds. These are usually set up for different financial objectives. You can contact a fund family by mail, telephone, or via the company's website. From there, they'll send you an application or a prospectus (many fund families let you download prospectuses online). Read the prospectus, then fill out the application and return it along with a check for your initial investment.

You can buy a mutual fund from a brokerage house or from the fund itself, and you may or may not be faced with a minimum initial investment. Another shopping option is known as a fund supermarket. This is a brokerage firm that lets investors select funds from a number of different fund families. Brokerage houses come in a variety of forms, from full-service houses that provide advice and guidance to deep discount brokerages. The downside to using a broker is that you'll generally pay a commission particularly if you use a full-service brokerage house.

While some invest the money in the fund of your choice, others put the money into an account and let it sit there until you've saved enough to reach their minimum investment level. This is the most direct-and cost-effective-way to buy shares in a mutual fund. All you need to do is contact the fund family and tell them you're interested in a particular fund.

Putting It All Together

The price of individual stocks can change constantly throughout a day of trading. Mutual funds are different. They receive only one price per day-at the end of each day's trading, based on what the securities in the portfolio are worth. The price per share, also known as the net asset value (NAV), of a mutual fund is the current market value of the fund's net assets divided by the number of *shares outstanding*. In most cases, that is the price that any investor pays to buy into the fund during the next day of trading.

Once you buy a fund, keep a close eye on it to see how it's performing. One way to do that is through a newspaper. Here, you can get information on daily price movements, annual rates of return, declaration of dividends, and other information. Many newspapers have the closing prices of the major funds. If you can't find yours, look in *The Wall Street Journal.*

If you have a financial software program on your PC, the job becomes much easier and potentially, more comprehensive. Many programs let you download quotes directly onto your computer. Over time, you can accumulate long-range data and statistics to

71

analyze how your fund is doing. Many online news sites let you look up your fund's activity for the day and other pertinent information using the fund's ticker symbol. A ticker symbol is a letter or series of letters that represent a stock or mutual fund. Although it's an easy trap to fall into, try not to pay undue attention to your fund's price movement every day. You're in this for the long haul, so watch long-term performance, not daily ups and downs.

Chapter 5

Investing in Bonds, CDs & MMFs

Bonds, CDs and MMFs are three of the safest places to invest your money

In this chapter that, we take a turn off the road that we've been following. As you know, mutual stock funds and individual stocks represent a form of ownership in companies. You buy shares in hopes that, as the companies prosper, so will your share of the pie. Bonds, certificate of deposits (CDs) and money market funds (MMFs) hold a different role in the investment world. They offer you an alternative and a form of balance that can lend stability and strength to a retirement portfolio.

Individual bonds and bond funds are vastly different entities. Individual bonds pay a fixed stream of income and return your principle on a specific date called the maturity date. Bond funds invest in many bonds with different interest rates and maturity dates. The fund's value varies daily and the income that's received from the bonds is distributed monthly to shareholders. It will vary month to month.

Bond Basics

Bonds are fancy IOUs. Companies and governments issue bonds to fund their day-to-day operations and to finance specific projects. Bonds can provide a worry-free stream of income. Handled with care, bond funds are among the most valuable tools in your 401(k) and IRA plans. However, don't invest all your retirement money in bonds. Inflation erodes the value of bonds' fixed interest payments.
When you buy a bond, you are loaning your money for a certain period of time to the issuer, be it General Electric or Uncle Sam. In return, bond holders get back their loan amount plus interest. Bond funds invest in many securities with different interest rates and coupon payments. The income received from the bonds is

73

distributed monthly to shareholders their 401(k) and IRA plans and the distribution varies as does the daily value of the fund.

Face value refers to the principal, the amount of money you invested when you bought the bond. It's also known as par value. A short-term bond is usually anything less than 3 years. Intermediate bonds can run from 4 years up to 12. Long-term bonds' terms last for 12 years and even longer. In general, the longer the term of the bond, the greater the interest that bond will pay its investors. The downside, of course, is that the longer the term of the bond, the longer you have to wait to get your initial investment back.

As a rule, bond values have an inverse relationship with interest rates. If interest rates go down, existing bonds can become more valuable. The reason is that newer bonds will be issued at a lower interest rate, making the older bond's higher rate that much more valuable. Here's an example of what can happen if you try to sell a bond before it reaches its maturity and interest rates are changing. Let's say you buy a 10-year corporate bond with a 6 percent yield. You pay $1,000, which means you'll earn $60 every year you continue to own the bond.

A year after you bought the bond, interest rates fall to 5 percent. At that level, you could probably sell your bond for about $1,100. That makes sense, since your 6 percent bond is worth more than the new ones coming out at 5 percent. Put that profit together with the $60 you earned in interest for one year, and that's a total profit of about 16 percent.

Corporate Bonds

Corporate bonds are issued by firms looking to raise money for any number of activities, from corporate expansion to underwriting development of a new product line. Yield is the effective rate of interest that a bond pays to investors. Many firms, in fact, prefer to raise cash via bonds in lieu of other options, such as issuing stock or seeking out a bank loan.

There are two distinct types of corporate bonds. The first is known as an investment grade bond. These, simply put, are the cream of the crop of the bond world. They are generally issued by large companies with impeccable financial credentials. As a result, these can be among the safest and most reliable bonds an investor can purchase. The other types of corporate bonds are known as junk bonds. In a way, that name is something of a misnomer. Rather than being worthless, junk bonds are issued by companies without the financial means to deal in investment-grade issues.

That classification cuts both ways. On the positive side for investors, given that junk bonds are seen as riskier than investment grade, their yield is often greater than that of investment grade. But, with junk bonds, since the firms issuing them lack the financial stability of investment-grade issuers, there's a chance that the companies will fail to payoff investors as the bonds specify.

Just how can you tell the difference between industrial class bonds and those with a greater degree of risk? Well, for one thing, the company issuing them should tell you something-a member of the Dow Jones 30 isn't as likely to put out bonds with a risk of default; a company with only a few years of operating history stands a better chance of doing that. But there's a more empirical way to do it. Bonds are rated by ratings agencies such as Moody's and Standard and Poor's. Each attaches a letter, which ranks the safety and credit solvency of the company issuing the bond. The system at Moody's is as follows:

Aaa Exceptional financial security.
Aa Excellent financial security
A Good financial security.
Baa Adequate financial security.
Ba Questionable financial security.
B Poor financial security.
Caa Very poor financial security.
Ca Extremely poor financial security.
Cb The worst of the worst. These are usually already in default.

For additional information behind what ratings mean, go to www.moodys.com. When it comes to finding suitable investments for your retirement, these ratings can prove a critical safety measure.

Unless you are operating from an extremely long time horizon with decades before you plan to retire, it's generally prudent to stick with higher-rated bonds with a greater certainty of safety. Know, too, that a bond's rating can change. For instance, Moody's or Standard and Poor's can drop a rating if a company suffers through a particularly harsh financial period. That, in turn, may suggest a bond that isn't quite as solid as you once believed. Generally, a rating of Baa or better is "investment grade." Below that is referred to as "junk" bonds that offer higher potential returns but also the greatest amount of risk. As a rule, it's best to avoid junk bonds for your retirement portfolio.

Treasury Bonds

One of the biggest advantages to treasuries in their varied forms is their security backed in full by the federal government. They are also exceedingly convenient to buy and levy no commission or sales charges. The downside is that returns can be rather modest. You may do just as well or even better with MMFs and CDs. And, like CDs, cash them in prior to their maturity date and penalties can accrue. For instance, you have to hold an I Bond for at least a year. If you redeem it before holding it five years, you forfeit three months' interest. For more information on treasury programs of all sorts, check out Treasury Direct at www.savingsbonds.gov. These are issued and backed by the federal government. They come in various forms and include:

Treasury Bills are government securities that can mature in a few days up to several weeks.

Treasury Notes are also government securities but with maturation as long as 10 years.

Treasury Bonds earn interest every six months.

I Savings Bonds are tied to inflation. If inflation goes up eroding the purchasing power of money, so does the amount an I Bond pays, protecting the value of the bond from inflation.

E and EE Savings Bonds. These pay interest based on current market rates and can mature as long as 30 years.

Although Treasury bonds have limited potential for serious appreciation, if they are well chosen, they can provide a steady flow of cash, which is shown in the table below. I have traditionally recommended almost no-risk Treasury bonds over corporate bond funds. High-quality corporate bond funds have only returned a half-percentage point more than Treasury bonds.

The U.S. Treasury's bonds are the safest bonds of all because the interest and principal payments are guaranteed by the "full faith and credit" of the U.S. government. Interest is exempt from state and local taxes, but not from federal tax when you take money out of your 401(k) plan. Because of their almost total lack of default risk, Treasury's bonds carry some of the lowest yields around and offer different maturity dates.

Zero Coupon Bonds

Zero coupon bonds offer an interesting twist so far as payback is concerned. They pay interest, but in a lump sum when the bond matures. The advantage to that is you can buy these bonds at a deep discount to 50 to 80 percent of their face value, depending on how long a maturity date the bonds carry. They can be particularly handy for funding your retirement. For instance, if you know a particular zero coupon bond will pay $10,000 when it matures in 20 years, you can plan on having that amount of money at that time. That makes zero coupons an effective retirement funding tool, since you know precisely what you can expect at a particular time. Moreover, you can buy several zero coupons with different maturity dates, thereby providing a structured, predictable flow of funds.

Municipal Bonds

Municipal bonds are issued by local and state governments. They help pay for a variety of municipal projects, including schools, highways, hospitals, housing, sewer systems, and other important public programs. One of the particular lures of municipal bonds to investors is that their return is exempt from federal taxes and, in many cases, state and local taxes as well. "Munis" (as they are known) actually come in two distinct forms.

General obligations municipal bonds are backed by the credit rating of the particular branch of the government that sells them to the public. These are generally considered very safe. Revenue bonds are generally sold for a specific project, such as building a highway or bridge. These are a bit less predictable because payback to investors depends on the project itself ultimately producing sufficient revenue to pay back those investors.

That raises a question: how should you choose between tax-free muni bonds and other sorts of bonds that may pay a higher rate of return? That depends on the bond's yield as well as your tax bracket. There's a simple formula that lets you make this calculation. Take the yield of a tax-free bond and divide it by one minus your tax rate. For example, a 4 percent municipal bond for someone in the 25 percent tax bracket would produce the taxable equivalent of 5.3 percent. Translated: go with any bond you may be considering that pays 5.3 percent or better. Anything less than that, and you're better off with the tax-free alternative.

International Bonds

These are bonds issued by companies based outside the United States. Like stocks, they can occasionally offer higher yields than domestic bonds. The downside is depending on the area of the world involved-greater political or economic instability. Additionally, there's the risk of the American dollar increasing in value versus foreign currencies. If that occurs, foreign bonds drop in value. A particularly large percentage of the foreign bond market is government bonds, as many countries do not have corporate bond markets developed to the extent that the United States does.

Guaranteed Investment Contracts

One final retirement funding option that is something of a variant on bonds is known as a Guaranteed Investment Contract, or GIC. These are issued by insurance companies or banks and are marketed to companies with defined contribution plans, such as 401(k)s. In fact, GICs have become a mainstay choice in a host of 40 1(k) plans. Like a bond, a GIC involves a promise that, having invested your money, you will receive a certain return within a specified period of time. Contracts can run up to five years and, like a bond, the interest rate is fixed. The upside to GICs is, as the name implies, your rate of return is guaranteed. The downside is your principal is not guaranteed, as it is with lesser paying options such as federal Treasury notes.

Bond Mutual Funds

When it comes time to plot out your investment strategy, you probably focus most of your attention on how equities are doing and pay scant attention to the inner workings of bonds. But as a word of caution, don't ignore the potential benefits of the fixed-income market. Trends in bond yields will often give you a better sense of the risks in the economy and your portfolio than stock funds can. Why? Equity investors are owners who care mostly about the upside potential of their holdings. Bond investors, by contrast, are creditors. They're worried about anything that could prevent them from getting paid back their money. So fixed-income investors are far more attuned to the current and near-term risks in the economy.

Bond funds are an excellent way to diversify your 401(k) and IRA plans with less money than what it costs to buy individual bonds. With whatever you want to spend, you can buy shares in a bond fund instead of spending a thousand dollars to buy one corporate bond. They often hold bonds from hundreds of companies, so you're shielded if a few companies default. By contrast, your returns suffer if you own a limited number of individual bonds from a handful of companies and an issuer defaults. You also get liquidity. You can sell fund shares any time at the fund's current value. Selling an individual bond often is tougher, if you must sell before maturity. They trade less frequently than stocks. And bonds typically trade "over the counter," meaning a broker hooks up buyers and sellers who negotiate price. Riskier bonds can be harder, and thus costlier, to unload.

When you buy shares in a bond fund, you are often holding bonds from hundreds of companies and government entities so you get diversification. By contrast, if you own a small number of bonds and a company defaults, your returns suffer. You can sell fund shares any time at the fund's current value. Selling individual bonds is more difficult if you want to sell before maturity, which is not a problem with bond funds. Be aware that bond funds charge management fees and some levy a sales charge when you buy or sell.

When interest rates are high, but you believe they'll go down, buy long-term bond funds. That's because when rates fall, longer-term bonds gain more in price than shorter-term bonds. So you win big scoring a large potential capital gain in addition to whatever interest the bonds in your fund are paying.

Interest payments on bonds are usually fixed and thus bond funds are known as "fixed-income" investments. Bond prices move in the opposite direction of interest rates. When interest rates fall, bond and bond fund prices rise, and vice versa. If you hold a bond to maturity, price fluctuations don't matter. You will get back the original face value of the bond, along with all the interest you expect. Don't invest all your retirement money in bonds. Inflation erodes the value of bonds' fixed interest payments. Stock returns, by contrast, stand a better chance of outpacing inflation. Despite the beating stocks sometimes take, young and middle-aged people should put a large chunk of their money in stocks. Even retirees should own some stocks, given that people are living longer than they used to.

Trends in bond yields will often give you a better sense of the risks in the economy than stock prices can. Why? Equity investors are owners who care mostly about the upside potential of their holdings. Bond investors, by contrast, are creditors. They're worried about anything that could prevent them from getting back their money. So fixed-income investors are far more attuned to the current and near-term risks in the economy.

Investing in CDs and MMFs

Certificate of deposits (CDs) are a popular choice for people who want total simplicity, no fees, and guaranteed principle plus interest at all times. They are typically issued on a three-month, six-month, one-year, or longer time basis. Short-term CDs (typically three to six months) pay slightly less interest than longer term CDs. If you purchase a CD, you are required to hold on to it until it expires (e.g., for three months or six months) or pay a small penalty for early withdrawal.

Money market funds (MMFs) are a special breed of savings account set up by financial institutions. They pay interest rates that are tied to the overall market interest rates. When you deposit money into an MMF account, your money begins to immediately earn interest at the current money market rate. And you can withdraw part or all of your deposit in an MMF at any time without incurring an early-withdrawal fee. The "no penalty" withdrawal feature gives the edge to MMFs and CDs. Both pay higher interest rates than passbook savings accounts. We cannot think of any reason why you would want to keep part or all of your savings in a passbook account over a CD or MMF.

Investments in CDs and MMFs are generally insured be the Federal Deposit Insurance Corporation (FDIC). The FDIC's coverage includes principal and interest through the date of the bank failure up to applicable insurance limit for each deposit. If a bank closes, interest ceases on all accounts. If another bank acquires the deposits from the failed bank, the acquiring bank becomes responsible for re-establishing interest rates and beginning the accrual of interest after the date of the failure of the bank. They may change the interest rate on the acquired deposits, but the depositor may withdraw their insured funds without penalty if they chose to do so. If no acquiring bank is found for the deposits and the FDIC pays the depositors directly for their insured amounts. You have the right to cash in your CD without penalty.

Putting It all Together

Bonds serve a different function than stock when it comes to providing a company with the financial means to grow. As we said earlier, a stock is a form of ownership. Not so with bonds. A bond is a form of loan. When you buy a bond, you're effectively entering into a contract with the issuer of that bond to pay whatever money you put up, plus interest. Each bond generally specifies just how often it will pay interest to investors, which is usually twice a year. On top of that, how much each payment comes to is also usually prearranged. Bonds also have a specified lifetime, which is also known as the "term." Once a bond reaches its term, investors have received the last of their interest payments and, at that point, also receive the face value of the bond.

Bonds are issued by companies, the federal government, and other local government agencies to fund all sorts of activities. They are rated according to their safety. The lower the ranking, the greater the potential payback, but the risk is greater as well. Bonds are also affected by interest rates. If rates go down, existing bonds go up in value because they pay more than bonds issued when rates are lower.

Bonds are also available in mutual fund form. Like stock funds, they offer diversity and professional management. GICs (Guaranteed Investment Contracts) are also a form of guaranteed payback. They are popular in 401(k) plans but don't offer the growth potential of stocks, but they can be useful for diversification and to balance the risks of stocks. A good place to park your investment money when the stock market takes a turn for the worst is in bonds, certificate of deposits (CDs) or money market funds (MMFs).

Chapter 6

Making Your Money Last

Do not squander your money because it's the stuff that retirement depends on

Making your money last is like planning a special dinner. You devise a menu, invite the guests, and map out a host of amenities to make sure everything goes as pleasantly as possible. But part of that process is setting the table, the place where everything is going to happen. If the table is poorly set, even the most sumptuous meal may seem like cheap takeout. The same goes for your retirement. You can know when you're going to retire and plan on how you hope to retire, but until you get some basics in place, even the most comprehensively mapped-out retirement may encounter unnecessary challenges. It comes down to a few basic financial steps that will not only make your current life all the more enjoyable, but set the financial stage for your retirement. Taken unto themselves, they're not particularly challenging or involved. But if they are ignored, they can undercut an otherwise solid retirement road map.

Making Money Last Basics

Do you find yourself carrying a credit card balance from one month to the next or worse, growing in size from month to month? Do you come to the end of the month with little or no money left over once all your necessary expenses have been paid? For substantial purchases, do you find yourself investigating payment plans rather than having sufficient cash on hand to meet the entire expense up front? Do you have a realistic sense of where your money goes and why?

These and similar questions may indicate money habits that are not as focused and well thought out as they might be. And it may also suggest a waste of funds that could be earmarked toward your retirement.

If you want to make your money last, you must start spending less. In order to do that, you must first know what you're spending now. Although this may sound like a no-brainer, many people don't fully comprehend that they spend more money than they make. How do you know what you are spending and money habits are as solid as they ought to be? The answer for many is setting up and following a budget. That may seem as pleasant as root canal work without anesthesia, but a budget is undeniably the most reliable way of planning where you spend your money as well as knowing just where your money actually goes.

Budgeting

Everyone should have a budget, even millionaires. It's crucial to know where your income is coming from and where it is going. By monitoring your spending habits, you will begin to identify areas where cost savings can occur. Your budget then becomes a valuable tool you can use to help you get out of debt, keep your spending on track, and find the extra money you need for your retirement plan. Many consider budgeting to be a tedious task, but it really doesn't have to be. Once you set your budget up, it can be easy and even fun to maintain.

One effective way to set up a budget that's right for you is to track your spending for a couple of months. Simply establish a list of fixed expenses as well as discretionary spending and follow the money trail. This is far more effective than trying to set up a budget based on recommended parameters a certain percentage for food, entertainment, and the like. A budget based on your requirements is bound to be more realistic-and, over the long haul, more effective. Important budget categories are:

Major expenses are usually contractual like rent and mortgage payments, car loans, property taxes, and day care. These are the expenses that you must pay before you consider your other expenses.

Necessities are important expenses such as groceries, utilities, and home maintenance that can be adjusted through tight money management techniques.

Credit card payments are the total monthly payments you need to make on all your cards.

Discretionary expenses can be significantly modified or eliminated altogether and include entertainment, take-out food, pocket money, etc.

Savings is the final component of the budget and shows what you'll do with any money that's left over after all expenses have been paid.

If you want to maintain your budget on your personal computer, there are several online sites that you can use like www.simpleplanning.net. Some banks also offer this service for their customers. If you don't have an expense-tracking system or don't like the one you're using, try the one at Yodlee.com or Mint.com to get started. There are several free online budgeting sites, such as Wesabe.com that can help you get through the budgeting process. LendingTree.com offers a "Money Right" option that will help you track what you're spending.

Whatever system you use should give you a quick picture of your overall expenses and make it easier to gain control over "out-of-control" expenses. This step is essential if you want to make room in your budget investing in your retirement. When you complete this process, you may be surprised to see exactly where your money is going each month. You'll discover places where you can cut back to come up with the money you need to save.

Once you are comfortable with your monthly budget, go through your list of expenses and check off those expenses that will likely go down when you retire such as commuting expenses and lunches at work. Next, mark those expenses that will likely go up when you retire like health care.

Sit down and analyze your money habits. If you've been consistently spending more than your budget allows, this breakdown should offer a comprehensive view of where the holes might be. While some spending is fixed and immune to change like a mortgage or car payments, or other discretionary spending can be prime targets for saving. For instance, one less lunch out a week can save $20 or so-that adds up to $1,000 a year. Getting books from the library rather than buying them, keeping an eye out for sales, and other strategies implemented in concert, can reap money-saving benefits.

We all know that impulse buying can put a huge dent in even the best mapped out budget. One strategy to ovoid this if you see that high definition television that you're sure you simply cannot go on living without, give your urge a week or two. Chances are good that, on further reflection, that plain old box you've been staring at these many years will seem more than adequate.

Ways to Spend Less

The following list will give you ideas about what you're spending and where to look for ways to spend less:

Lower your insurance premiums. Shop around for less expensive auto, home, and life insurance policies. If you have low-deductibles, find out how much you would save by increasing your deductibles. Going for a $250 to $500 deductible on car collision insurance can save you 20 percent of more. Don't over insure.

Reduce your telephone and television expenses. Switching from an unlimited calling plan to one that offers you a fix number of minutes per month is one way to reduce your monthly telephone bill. Cut the premium television channels you never watch.

Cut your grocery bill. Shop once a week because the more trips you make to the store, the more likely you are to buy tempting impulse items. Stop drinking bottled water and instead, buy a filter for your faucet. Buy only food that's in season. Out-of-season produce can cost 25 to 50 percent more.

Cut your gasoline bill. Drive to work with a colleague or matchup with someone at www.carpoolworld.com or www.erideshares.com. Burn regular gas instead of premium if your car will accept regular. Check your owner's manual. Check your owner's manual. Combine trips or ride your bike.

Cut your cleaning costs. Most clothes that are dry cleaned can be washed by hand or in a washing machine.

Trim your kids' college expenses. College books cost a fortune if bought new. Rent them for a fraction of cost new books from www.campusbookretals.com or www.chegg.com.

Negotiate lower credit card rates. Call your credit card customer service and tell them you're planning to transfer your balance unless they give you a lower rate. Compare rates at www.cardratings.com or www.billshrink.com.

Reduce your energy bills. If your utility company offers it, get a free energy audit on your home or do it yourself using the guide at www.energystar.gov. Set a programmable thermostat that you can buy for under $50 to automatically lower the heat or raise the temperature of the air conditioner after bedtime and when you're not home. Use florescent bulbs that use 75 percent less energy and last 10 times longer than incandescent ones.

Shop online. If you want to buy a high-end item without having to pay a high-end price, shop online at www.bluefly.com, www.yoox.com or www.ebay.com. There are numerous other reputable sites that are out there. Many local retailers will match internet prices rather than lose your business.

Have fun for a lot less. Go to a minor-league ball game and you'll probably pay 20 percent of what it would have cost you for major-league tickets. Cut back on eating out and eliminate fast-food places from your menu.

Watch how you use credit cards. Pay with cash or use a debit card your everyday purchases like groceries. Create a payoff plan for each of your credit cards. When you pay off a card, cut it in half and cancel it. When you start paying with cash, you'll find yourself passing up impulse purchases.

Automatically save any extra money you get. When you get a raise, deposit the extra amount of money you get directly into a savings account so you'll never miss it. Do the same thing with part-time money, bonuses, or overtime pay. When you get an income tax refund, use it to pay off a credit card. Then cancel the card and deposit the money you were paying on the card into your savings account.

Reducing little expenses can add up quickly, so be creative at finding the money you're wasting. Make gradual changes that are easier to stick with. Start taking lunches to work instead of eating out and you'll be amazed at how much you'll save. You'll also feel a lot better. Have raises and bonuses automatically deposited into a savings account. If you finally paid off your car loan and there's still several years left in the old clunker, invest what you were paying into an installment loan.

Getting Rid of Debt

Setting up and following a budget and reigning in your use of credit cards are two powerful ways to get your financial house in order- and, in so doing, free up money that can be set aside for retirement. Many people might assume that these forms of discretionary spending are the primary targets for cost savings. Not necessarily. Other, more fixed costs can also prove lucrative savings sources, provided you know where to look and what to take advantage of and what to avoid.

Should you save money or pay off your debts first? A lot of people aren't in the enviable position of having the financial ability to do both. The die-hard savers will argue that the more money they have in savings, the better they can survive a financial emergency without running up more debt. The opposing debt-killers will argue that the amount of interest they'll earn in a savings account is insignificant in comparison to the interest they're paying on loans. Who's right?

Both are. However, everyone needs to develop the discipline it takes to save even if it's a small amount while you're paying off your debts.

Some financial advisors will encourage you to pay off smaller debts first regardless of the interest rates to reduce your number of debts faster. Others say you should consider consolidating all of your credit cards onto one that offers you a balance transfer option. However, the consolidation option opens you up to the temptation of adding more debt to the very cards that got you in trouble in the first place. It makes financial sense to pay off your higher interest rate debts first because those are the ones that are costing you the most.

To get started, organize your outstanding loans from the highest to the lowest interest rate. If you are able to do it, increase the amount of your payments against your high interest rate loans first to get them paid off. Then once a loan is paid off, use that money to increase the payment you're making on you next highest interest rate loan. There are a number of repayment plan calculators online at websites like www.quicken.com. It offers a debt Reduction Planner that is an excellent get-out-of-debt planning tool. Similar tools are available in personal finance software applications that are available at your local computer supply store for about $25 to $50.

Credit Cards

When you pay off a high-interest credit card, destroy it. After you've cut it up into small pieces, three wonderful things will happen. First, you'll start buying less of what you really don't need. According to a recent study, credit cards account for over 50 percent of the impulse-buying patterns of shoppers. Second, your total debt will start to shrink exponentially. As high-interest cards get paid off, you will end up with money you didn't know you had for investing into your 401(k) or IRA accounts. Finally, once you're out of debt, you will feel great. Keep just one or two cards to cover yourself for financial emergencies only. When you can consistently pay the balance off at the end of each month, you will know you've kicked the credit card habit for good.

For many, the heart of spending issues is credit card use and abuse. It's not surprising-credit cards are plentiful, relatively easy to obtain, and often exceedingly generous in the amount of credit they afford their users. On the surface, that may suggest a wealth of financial potential, but that potential far too often causes problems. The American Bankers Association reports that the average American household owes $9,000 on credit cards. That would be bad enough unto itself, but couple that amount with the sting of ongoing interest charges can easily top 15 percent or more and you have a growing problem.

Many cardholders only see one number on their monthly statement (the minimum payment). This usually represents roughly 2.5 percent of the balance you owe, is the absolute least you have to pay that particular month. In the case of the $8,000 average cited above, that comes to a modest $200. The trouble is, paying the minimum is little more than treading water, financially speaking. The minimum basically buys you another month-while interest continues to accrue on the remaining balance. For example, paying the $200 minimum on an $8,000 balance on a 13 percent interest card will take 263 months or nearly 22 years to pay off the entire sum. Even worse, you'll pay nearly $2,600 in interest alone.

How does this all relate to planning your retirement? For one thing, excessive credit card debt is yet another hole draining cash away from your retirement goals. For another, it's a habit you don't want to carry with you into your retirement. Trying to enjoy life on a fixed amount of money can prove downright perilous if interest charges are steadily eating away at your nest egg.

That makes sensible credit card management another retirement prerequisite that warrants your attention. If credit card abuse is of concern to you, here are some strategies to bring it under control-and, in the process, better position you for retirement. Don't carry a wallet full of cards. Ubiquitous as credit card offers can be, there's rarely a need to carry more than two cards (one for regular use, the other for emergencies). If you have substantial balances on more than one card, choose the one with the highest interest rate and begin paying that down as aggressively as possible.

If you carry a large balance on a card with a hefty interest rate, another option is transferring the balance to another card-one that often levies no interest charges for as long as a year or so. But, if that appeals, commit to paying down the transferred balance as fast as possible. Sooner or later, interest on the new card will spike. This is known as a *teaser card*. It's an apt name since interest rates on teaser cards often jump to high levels, often much more expensive than other cards that don't offer the introductory carrot of no interest. If you carry balances on several high rate cards, look into consolidating that debt into one card. That can lower your payments, not to mention making the task of paying down your debt a bit simpler.

Money Savings Strategies

Let's assume you've been able to trim your expenses, you've got a budget that works, your debt is manageable, and your housing expenses are as modest as anyone could hope for. Now it's time to consider how to best handle all that cash you've freed up. Unfortunately, keeping your money in a conventional savings or checking account isn't a whole lot better than stuffing the cash into the mattress. While many checking accounts pay no interest whatsoever, as of this writing, conventional interest-bearing checking accounts were averaging less than 1 percent. Still, there is some good news: as is the case with all bank deposits, your money is insured by the federal government through the Federal Deposit Insurance Corporation (FDIC).

Fortunately, there are alternatives to run-of-the-mill savings accounts. One worth investigating is Internet based checking and savings accounts. These can pay higher interest than conventional savings. Although it is possible to earn something with these sorts of interest-bearing checking accounts, there are drawbacks. First, many banks mandate substantial minimums to open such accounts. By the same token, other banks have low minimums to open an account but require that you maintain hefty minimums to avoid monthly fees. For instance, one bank lets you open an account with a skinny

$25, but requires an average $1,000 without incurring fees. Other options that offer quick access to cash:

Money market deposit accounts are offered by banks and, like savings accounts, are FDIC insured. They also pay slightly higher interest than conventional savings. The downside is that minimums to open an account can be high and many accounts limit the number of transactions.

Money market funds are offered by brokerage houses and mutual fund families. Since they invest in relatively safe choices such as government securities, their return is reasonable and commonly top 5 percent interest. However, they are not FDIC insured.

Earning Extra Money

Yes, you are working hard to meet your retirement goal, but sometimes the only way you can get there is to earn some extra money. According to the Bureau of Labor Statistics, 4 out of 10 Americans are working a second job. Moonlighting – holding a second job in addition to a regular one can take on many different forms. Looking for a part-time job is much like the steps you went through to find your full-time job. Scan the classified job ads and surf the job boards on the Internet for leads. Be sure to check out the temporary services as well. When the regular job market is weak, the temporary job market can compensate for the difference. Temporary services cut across all occupations and time slots around the clock.

40 Great Home Businesses For Baby Boomers is a great book published by Western Publications (www.Westernpubs.com.) and it's complete with cost and earnings estimates. It will even help you create a dynamic business plan for your home business. You need to identify your target market with a clear definition of who will most likely be your customer – the ones who will buy your products or services. Decide how you will reach them (i.e., advertisements) and how you will sell to them. Your plan should include a three-year cash flow projection showing monthly estimates for income, expenses, and profits.

Always have a separate telephone number and email address for your home business. You won't impress potential or existing customers who call and get an answer from a family member that is not associated with your business. Use a separate email address that identifies the name of your business rather than your own name. Your business must be able to accept payment from Visa and Master cards. Yes, you will have to pay a service fee, but you don't want to turn down a sale because you can't accept a customer's card.

If you have a limited background in accounting, then get a good accountant to help you out, even if you have to pay for it. An accountant can show you how to keep track of your income and expenses and potentially save you thousands of dollars by taking legitimate tax deductions. Keep your accounting records straight by keeping receipts for all business expenses.

Diversifying Your Assets

There are two important reasons to have an asset diversification plan. First, it is easier to predict what the future performance of your overall portfolio will be by studying the historical performance of the current news that may be the way chosen to diversify assets. The important reason for your diversification plan is that it ensures that you own a variety of investment categories. The idea behind diversification is to reduce risk while increasing your expected returns. If one of your selections is going down, others are hopefully going up to offset it.

Ensuring that you have the mix of investment that is appreciating in value is an important part of having a retirement plan. The mix in your portfolio will change as you get older. It's based on the eventual results you're looking for and your time frame. You periodically adjust it to suit the amount of risk you're willing to take. Deciding on what's the right mix for you is a relatively simple task once you know how it's done and what's involved. For example, you don't want a portfolio that is too risky or one that's not aggressive enough to grow.

Each investment category (i.e., stock funds, bond funds, etc.) is influenced by different market and economic factors. Stocks typically do better during one part of the market cycle, while bonds do better in another. This is one of the reasons why your allocation plan is so important. If you understand how basic market factors affect your mix of investments, you are in a better position to reallocate your assets to take whatever action is appropriate to the ups and downs of the market.

For example, let's assume you're comfortable with accepting some risk in your portfolio and have selected a mix of 75 percent stocks and 25 percent bonds. Market forces begin to favor bond returns and are driving stock prices down. You rebalance your portfolio mix by selling some of your stock funds to buy bond funds to obtain a 50/50 percentage allocation mix. When the situation reverses itself and the economic forces begin to favor stocks, you sell some of your bond holdings at a profit and buy cheap stocks that are on their way up. By periodically rebalancing your mix whenever the economy dictates, you will be buying investments at low prices and selling at high prices.

Managing a mix of investment on a recurring basis gives you an opportunity to rebalance your portfolio, improving the mix. For example, you may decide to sell assets that have done well and use the cash to buy other investments that are trading at low prices. Two of the best online asset allocation tools are www.dinkytown.com and www.calcxml. Both help you determine an investment mix based on your time horizon and tolerance for risk. There is an online asset allocation questionnaire that will help guide you to proper asset allocation for your retirement portfolio. It's available at www.smartinvestmentbook.com.

Consider an Annuity

The word annuitizes means that you take a fixed sum of money and convert it into a series of regular payments. You can purchase an annuity from insurance companies and some brokerage firms to annuitize the money you paid for the annuity. Annuity payments are offered for a lifetime or over a specified time period. Installment payments are made for a set amount over a specified period of time like 5, 10, or more years.

A life annuity pays you for as long as you live. Joint annuities pay you and another person (i.e., spouse) through the end of the longer of the two lifetimes. Single-life annuities pay you a stipulated amount on a regular basis (i.e., monthly) until you die. Annuity with spousal benefits pays you a stipulated amount on a regular basis until you die and then pays your spouse a stipulated amount on a regular basis until they die.

Recurring annuities pays you and your spouse a stipulated amount on a regular basis until you or your spouse dies and continues paying the same amount until the remaining spouse dies. Many 401(k) providers offer annuity options to participants in their plans. Most of the major life insurance companies offer annuity products.

Consider a Reverse Mortgage

On the surface, a reverse mortgage sounds like a "can't lose" deal for older homeowners who are about to retire. A lender gives you what amounts to a cash advance on your home equity and you don't have to pay it back until you move or die. At that time, the lender sells the home and uses the proceeds from the sale of your home to close out the loan. Reverse mortgages are particularly appealing to retirees looking to supplement their limited retirement income. You have to be at least 62 to qualify for a reverse mortgage.

There are some serious drawbacks to reverse mortgages if it's an option that you're considering. You can expect to pay high fees to get a reverse mortgage. In addition to regular closing costs, you'll pay an origination fee of 2 percent or more on the first $200,000 of the loan and 1 percent or more thereafter. You'll also be required to pay a mortgage insurance premium of about 2 percent plus a monthly service charge as well. By the time you add all the fees together, fees can easily reach $10,000 or more.

The formula for determining your loan amount takes into account your age, the current interest rates, as well as your home's value.

Anything you owe on your home is subtracted from that amount, as are all loan fees. The older you are, the more you can borrow. To see how much you might qualify for, use the calculator at www.Revmort.com/nrmla.

Before you can get a reverse mortgage, you'll be required to attend a session with a financial counselor who is not affiliated with the lender. Before you sign up for one, make sure you understand all the risks that are involved with reverse mortgages. Look into all the alternatives that you may have such as cutting expenses, taking out a home-equity line of credit or down-sizing your home.

Moving out of a large home that you needed when you were raising the kids and into something that's less expensive is a perfect way to free up some money instead of getting a reverse mortgage. If you don't plan to live in your current home when you retire, so much the better. Unmarried homeowners are allowed to realize $250,000 in capital gains when they sell their primary residence. If you're married, you get double that amount or $500,000. You can then take your time to explore the places you might want to retire without have to commit to the expense of owning another home.

Consider Retiring Mortgage Free

Buying a home is the most significant financial obligation most of us carry. With regard to planning for your retirement, owing as little as possible on your home is advantageous on several levels. First, paying off your mortgage as quickly as possible eliminates a significant financial load that much sooner. By the same token, should you decide to sell your home at any point-prior to or after retiring your *equity* will be that much greater. And that means a greater overall profit.

Equity refers to the difference between the value of your home and the amount you owe on your mortgage. For instance, a $300,000 home with a remaining mortgage of $175,000 results in equity of $125,000. Surprised at how much even a small extra payment can do to

cut both the life of your mortgage as well as the overall cost? It's simple-every conventional payment you make goes to pay both interest and principal. Anything extra goes directly toward paying down the principal-and, over time, cutting both the overall life of the loan as well as the
amount owed.

On the surface, paying off a mortgage that can easily reach into hundreds of thousands of dollars may seem insurmountable. And, in many cases, paying off a mortgage completely is, in fact, unrealistic. But you can pay down a good chunk of the mortgage rather painlessly-and, in the process, save yourself thousands of dollars in interest costs.

Here's a quick calculation to illustrate how this works. Say you take out a $150,000 30-year mortgage at 6 percent interest. That means a monthly payment of $899. Under that arrangement, paying off the loan over the full 30 years means interest payments totaling more than $173,000-more than the cost of the loan itself! However, tacking on a modest $50 a month to your payment lets you pay off the loan 4 years sooner and, in the process, save some $26,000 in interest.

One misleading aspect to the "average" closing costs is that expenses differ significantly from one area of the country to another-not to mention one lender to another. For instance, in the Bankrate.com survey, New York was at the top of the list in terms of closing expenses-$3,887. Halfway across the country, Missouri checked in with the cheapest at $2,713. So make sure you know your closing costs to make certain the refinance is worth it. Upping that to an extra $100 per month pays off the loan in only 23 years and saves some $45,000 in interest.

Putting It all Together

What this entire chapter boils down to is the importance of retirement planning and the consistent execution of a financial plan. Without a thoughtful strategy in place and the means to follow through on that plan, the notion of retirement becomes a far more haphazard proposition than it needs to be. As we've discussed in this chapter, the responsibility for mapping out and executing a financial plan for retirement is increasingly an issue of personal responsibility rather than an employer "taking care" of retirees. With the ball so squarely in your court, it's critical that you approach that duty with a plan that takes into consideration both your goals for retirement as well as the reality of your situation.

As we proceeded through the chapter, we introduced to comprehensive details about the specific steps that comprise an effective, thoughtful plan. Your plan needs to take in more than just financial considerations. Money is critical to retirement, but so is an idea of how you intend to spend your time at something that's rewarding and enjoyable-not mere filler. Start early to give you the best chance to put together the best financial package possible, allows for adequate time for any necessary adjustments along the way and can help ease some of the pressures that can accompany planning for your retirement.

It's never too late to catch up. By the same token, you may be a somewhat older person with little in the way of retirement planning or resources in place. There's always time to think about your retirement and from there, build and execute a program that can help you catch up in a hurry.
You may think you have the most thoughtful, comprehensive financial plan around. That may be so, but be sure to monitor your progress. Few are the plans that prove successful from a "set it and forget it" approach. Know where you are and where you're going at every step along the way.

Don't be afraid to adjust things as need be. Circumstances change, as do your goals and wishes. As you proceed toward retirement, don't be gun-shy about making adjustments, be it to the financial makeup of your plan or your long-term objectives. Nothing to do with your retirement needs to be cast in stone.

Chapter 7

Retirement Action Items

*Action happens only when you consistently move one
foot ahead of the other*

One of the biggest fears people have when it comes to retirement is
financial. According to Forbes Magazine, most retirees fail to meet
their monthly expenses within the first year after they retire. That's
because they didn't have a plan and set specific goals for their
401(k) and IRA plans before they retired. Be careful not to fall into
the same trap. The potential pitfalls to retirement is letting it happen
and hoping that something, somehow, will appear to engage you for
the remaining years of your life. When planning the financial
elements of your retirement, don't spare any detail as to just what all
that money is going to do for you in terms of continuing a fulfilling,
rewarding life. If you're getting ready to transition out of your job
and into retirement, there are a number of things to consider.

Have you developed a solid set of retirement goals that you have
either met, or are in the process of meeting to accomplish you
retirement? Do you know how much money you'll need to support a
retirement lifestyle that's acceptable to you? Have you identify the
sources of retirement income that you expect to receive after you
retire? Do you have any dependents that you must take care of after
you retire? If yes, how will you handle this? If you retire before you
are eligible for Medicare, do you have medical insurance to cover
yourself? We'll help you answer these questions in this chapter.

What to Do Right Away

Life is full of risks. You could die, wreck your car, become disabled,
burn your house down, have a catastrophic medical expense, get
sued, or need long-term care. Anyone of these can de-rail the best
retirement plan. Fortunately, you can hedge against all these
disasters, at tolerable cost, through insurance. By sharing these risks
with many people, you can guard against the flying fickle finger of

fate, and protect your future plans. Make sure you are insured to the point where the risk, should it occur, won't disrupt your retirement plans.

Unfortunately, retirees often postpone making the necessary preparations that will allow their wishes to be granted and their family looked after until it is too late. Their reaction is the same as the authors of most financial planning books: "Maybe if I don't think about this stuff, nothing bad will happen." Don't be one of those people. At the very minimum, every retiree should have the following instruments in place a will, living trust, and durable power of attorney.

Today, is anybody ever sure that they won't lose their job, be involved in an accident, or need to replace their roof? This is why it's so important to have an emergency fund set aside. This is money you can get your hands on immediately. How much do you need depends on your job, your health, your ability to tap credit lines, insurance, and other individual considerations. We would recommend three to six months of after-tax income at a minimum, with more if you are the type to see the glass as half empty. Emergency funds can keep an annoying event from
turning into a financial disaster.

Clearly, your emergency stash is part of the savings you have outside of your retirement funds, but there could be big expenditures you want to make: a wedding to pay for; a once-in-a-lifetime-trip, or whatever. Although we are adamant about the need to save for retirement, we don't want you to put your life on hold until then. You can't forego every expense until after your retire. So, how do you balance pre- and post-retirement needs? Here's our suggestion. After you have your emergency fund filled to the maximum, start dividing your savings this way: Put 90% toward your retirement and the rest to your emergency fund savings.

We can't save for you from not saving. Only you can make that happen. However, we can tell you that if you don't save, no matter how many investment books you read, you will still end up destitute. Even if you have the world's best investment advisor, you are still going to be broke if you don't contribute generously to your retirement accounts. Create an autopilot savings plan. Set a savings goal and have that money automatically taken out of your paycheck and put into an investment account such as your 401(k) or IRA. They are an extremely powerful retirement planning tools in their own right. If you are not taking advantage of what they have to offer, your retirement planning has a significant hole in it. Accumulate assets for retirement by funding your 401(k) and IRA plans annually.

Take advantage of compound interest. Time is such a valuable commodity, so don't squander it. Yet many retirees do, wasting a resource that can't ever be recovered. Time is an investor's most valuable ally. Returns increase exponentially over time, which is as close to magic as most of us will ever see. Putting time on your side is a key element to financial success. As you get closer to retirement, you will want to shift into more conservative investments, because you will have less time to recover from market meltdowns such as the one we experienced in 2008. We describe the shift from equities to bonds and cash that occurs over time as your guide. Use low-cost financial services companies such as Vanguard and Schwab and Fidelity, and discount brokers such as Scottrade and TD Ameritrade for your investments.

Activating Social Security

Social Security's problems are well documented, and surveys show that many people who are not yet retired do not expect to receive much from Social Security. For many retirees, however, Social Security is a key source of income, and it probably will continue to be for many years despite all the negative headlines. For lower-income workers, Social Security benefits replace up to 90 percent of their pretax working years' income.

Social Security is a valuable asset for retirees. Few people, however, know as much as they should about Social Security, and many aspects of the program are not automatic. Each beneficiary decides when retirement benefits begin, and that choice affects the amount that is received. The choices made can affect one's spouse and other family members. Recipients also can influence how much of the benefits are taxed and whether any of the benefits are lost because the recipient continues to earn income from working. To maximize Social Security benefits, some key decisions have to be made.

Social Security benefits can be managed to maximize their value. That's because the program provides options that can increase or reduce benefits. Benefits also might be subject to income taxes. In the following sections we'll examine the key issues affecting Social Security benefits and develop methods for making the best choices. Deciding when to take your Social Security benefit is an important part of your retirement program and your long-term financial security. You can currently draw reduced benefits from the program at age 62 and full benefits at 65 if you were born before 1937. The age limit gradually creeps up to 67 if you were born after that time. Given the problems that we covered in the trustee's report, you can expect the age limits will continue to move up.

Check out www.socialsecurity.gov/estimator to get an estimate of your benefit or contact your local Social Security office at least six months before you want your benefits to start to get the latest information. If you decide to take your benefit before you quit working, there are limits on how much work income you can earn without a penalty. You're currently required to give back $1 for every $2 you earn over the earnings limit. Check with the Social Security website at www.socialsecurity.gov to find out what the current limits are.

Signing Up for Medicare

The financial crisis that Medicare faces is far greater than Social Security. Medicare's Hospital Insurance trust fund will be depleted over the next 5 years. Since the late 1980s, the government budget has been combining the "actuarial surplus" in a Medicare fund. Thus, the current multi-trillion dollar budget deficit is consuming almost every bit of that "surplus" that was supposed to be paying for the baby boomers' medical care.

102

Health care is a wild card in any retirement budget. The average retiree spends anywhere from $2,500 to $6,000 annually on out-of-pocket medical expenses. The estimates include all costs, such as Medicare and insurance premiums, deductibles, copayments, and non-covered expenses. But it is just an average. A particular retiree might spend more or less, depending on health, family history, and insurance coverage. The amount increases above the average as the retiree ages. Study the medical expense coverage options carefully before estimating retirement expenditures. Make sure you know exactly what is and what is not covered including prescription drugs by Medicare or any private insurance you may have. Determine what your part is of any co-pay requirements. Typically, Medicare pays 80 percent and you pay 20 percent.

Regardless of when you decide to take your Social Security benefit, you must apply for Medicare health insurance at age 65. The aging of the baby boomers will put a strain on health insurance premiums including Medicare. You can expect the cost for health care will continue to go up annually. This can and probably will be a drain on your retirement savings. That combined with a lengthening life span for Americans demand that you consider all aspects of your personal health care in your retirement plan.

Unfortunately, there isn't anything you can do about the prospect of increased Medicare rates that will come directly out of your monthly social security check. However, some aspects of your health care are within your control. Maintain a good weight by limiting the junk food you eat, exercise regularly, quit smoking and drinking, and see your doctor at least once a year for an annual checkup are ways you can reduce your risk of high medical costs in retirement.

Minimizing Your Taxes

Don't assume that your taxes will be lower once you retire and stop earning taxable wages. Unfortunately, this may not always be the case. Economists have consistently warned that tax rates may go up to cover the federal deficit. If your retirement accounts are invested in tax-deferred plans, then you'll owe income taxes on the withdrawals. If you elected to convert some or all of your tax-deferred plans to tax-free plans, then your tax liability will be less. A part of everyone's social security income is taxable, and withdrawals from most retirement plans are taxable as well. And, with the massive buildup of federal and some state budget deficits, tax rate could increase by the time you retire.

Should you pay taxes now or pay later? Taxes play a big part of retirement planning particularly if you're nearing retirement. Arranging the investments in your retirement accounts to take advantage of the tax laws while you are working and after you retire is a consideration. Income and capital gains taxes will go up in the future to cover the multi-trillion dollar national deficit. Although you can't do anything about that, you can use the time you've got before you retire to take advantage of tax-saving options that are available to you – taxable, tax-differed, and tax-free accounts. Make sure you know what income tax bracket you're in by visiting the IRS website at www.irs.gov. You can use www.completetax.com to help you project your future taxes.

Capital gain rates are lower than income tax rates and affect the stock part of your assets. Investments such as money market accounts and bond funds are mostly taxed at income tax rates and should be concentrated in tax-sheltered accounts like your 401(k) and IRA. For example, if you've allocated 50 percent of your assets for retirement in stocks and 50 percent in bonds and money market accounts, ideally you would have most of your stocks in taxable accounts where you can take advantage of lower capital gain tax rates and the rest of your funds held in retirement accounts.

Estimating Your Cash Flow

For you non-accounts, cash flow is an accounting exercise where you identify the sources of cash you've got coming in and how you plan to apply that cash to specific expenses. The techniques you use to determine your cash flow are similar to the steps you went through to prepare a budget. You start by reviewing your regular monthly living expenses like food, utilities, and mortgage payments to determine how much cash you'll need to cover those expenses.

The next step is to determine what your non-monthly will be for things like property taxes, insurance payments, car maintenance, and travel over the for the next twelve months. Then total these expenses and divide them by twelve to convert them to an estimated monthly expense. The final step in the cash flow is to determine what your monthly income will be from sources like Social Security and monthly pension payments. The following example shows what your cash flow requirement might look like in a table.

Estimate of Retirement Cash Flow			
Income & Expenses	Items Covered	$/Mon	$/Year
Monthly Income	Social security, pension, 401(k) withdrawal, etc.		
Non-Monthly Income	Tax refunds, personal loans, etc.		
Sub-Total			
Monthly Expenses	Rent, mortgage payments, utilities, food, car related expenses, credit cards, etc.		
Non-Monthly Expenses	Property taxes, insurance premiums, medical bills, travel, etc.		
Sub-Total			
Total Cash Needed			

The total of the monthly income needs to be less than the monthly expense and the non-monthly expense prorated to a monthly amount. That's because emergencies and unplanned for expenses will occur when you retire just as when you were working. To keep these unplanned expenses from draining your retirement accounts, put your surplus money in a saving account that you can draw on to cover unexpected expenses.

If you need to withdraw money from a retirement account like your 401(k), make sure it's an amount that you're comfortable with. For example, if you have $50,000 in your account and based on your total monthly expenses, you need an additional $500 a month out of your 401(k) to cover your expenses, then you will be using-up one percent of your 401(k) to meet your cash flow needs. That means that over the next 100 months (100 months X $500 = $50,000), your 401(k) OR IRA will dwindle down to zero dollars. That assumption assumes that it's not invested in anything. However, if it is invested in assets that on average are realizing a compound annual interest rate of 12% or $6,000 per year, then your retirement accounts are meeting your cash flow needs without losing any value.

Consider Relocating

If you're thinking about relocating after you retire in the hopes of enjoying milder weather and lower expenses, make sure you first assess the overall tax burden of potential sites. Some states that are currently tax-friendly could get a lot less tax-friendly as they scramble to find new sources of revenue to plug gaping holes in their recession-shredded budgets.

Although your federal taxes won't change where ever you live, your state and local taxes can vary significantly from one location to another. If you itemize deductions, how much you pay in local property taxes for the same house in different states can vary widely. Where to Retire magazine (www.wheretoretire.com) offers a state-by-state tax guide, including special exemptions for seniors and a rundown of how various types of retirement income are taxed. Kiplinger Magazine offers an interactive retiree tax map on their website at www.kiplinger.com/links/retireetaxmap.

If you bought your home years ago, chances are you've ended up with an asset that's worth more than what you paid for it. And if you have paid off the mortgage, it could be the cornerstone of your retirement nest egg. The opportunity to leverage the equity you've built up is something you should think about. As you approach retirement, there are several options to consider when you evaluate whether you should keep or sell your home.

Consider trading down, particularly if you feel that you won't need the size of home you're living in now when you retire. What will it cost to get an acceptable smaller replacement? If the potential profit from selling your home is minimal, it might not be worth the effort to relocate before or after you retire.

Time the sale of your home to take advantage of the tax breaks. If you or your spouse is fifty-five or older, you can exclude from taxes up to $500,000 of the capital gain on the sale of your home. You may want to consider selling your home and moving to a part of the country where the cost of housing and living are lower. Not only will you get more home for your money, you will get the added benefit of a lower cost of living in a new area.

Controlling Inflation

One of the reasons behind interest bearing assets in your 401(k) and IRA plans is to make sure your retirement income keeps up with inflation. There are several steps you can take that will help you deal with inflation. Annually track your expenses in an online inflation calculator like www.mint.com or www.yodlee.com so that you can see how inflation is affecting you. The percentage your expenses have increased over last year is your personal inflation rate.

Fortunately, inflation has been relatively tame over the past decade. But, watch out because it could become a significant factor as we move into the second decade of the 21st century. The huge accumulation of trillions of dollars in federal debt over the last couple of years is in and of itself, inflationary. Our spendthrift government has to either borrow more money to pay for the deficit or significantly increase taxes. If they take the easy way out and borrow the money, that will drive the cost of loans (i.e., interest rates) up for everybody including American business up that adds to their cost of producing the products and services we consume.

Who's going to pay for it? You got it – higher prices will be passed on to consumers.

And the resulting high inflation will be detrimental to the health of the economy and your retirement to say the least. It erodes the buying power of money, which is particularly bad for retirees on fixed incomes. Inflation is usually not a problem when the economy is weak, which is the one good thing about recessions. Retail spending plunges and unemployment is up, which takes pressure off prices. And, of course, increases in the price of oil are readily visible to you at the gas pump. Its inflationary impact immediately hit your pocket book.

Planning for price increases of the thing you buy as a result of inflation should be taken into consideration when you calculate how much you'll need when you retire. The inflation rate is measured by the government in what's called the Consumer Price Index (CPI) that is reported on a regular basis in the financial section of newspapers and on the news media. Pay close attention to the CPI because it's one way to gauge how your living expenses might be changing (i.e., up or down). Increases in the cost of home maintenance and medical care are two expenses that can adversely affect your retirement savings.

Hard Choices to Consider

Sometimes cutting back on what you're spending is all you need to do to get ready for retirement. If that doesn't make a big enough dent to help you make ends meet, you may need to look at some major items that are costing you the most money. You may have to make some hard choices now if you want to retire. If you haven't been able to bring your expenses in line with your retirement income, the question is not whether you are going to have to make hard choices, but rather which hard choices are you going to make.

Is your car sabotaging your ability to make ends meet? If it is, do you really need it after you retire? In the interim, is there a cheaper way for you to get back and forth to work each day? There probably is if you think about it. If you're willing to get rid of your car, you could save hundreds of dollars on payments, upkeep, gasoline, and insurance. If you can't survive without a car, consider selling it and getting a cheaper one that will get you from point A to point B just fine, with less luxury.

If you make it this far in the book and you still have no idea of what you need to do to get out of debt, consider getting help from a credit counselor. They can put you in a debt management program if they're willing to accept you as a client. Your counselor will arrange for you to pay off your debts usually at a lower interest rate. In exchange, In exchange, you have to agree to stop using your credit cards and applying for additional credit. From this point, you make one payment (usually monthly) to your counselor who in turn pays your creditors. If you break the agreement, you will be removed from the program. If you're interested in this is a program, start your search for a counselor at www.simpleliving.net and www.debetorsanonymous.org.

If your personal debt is escalating to the point where you're having trouble paying even the minimum on your debts and collecting agencies are hounding you, then you need to take some hard action right now because it probably won't get any better when you stop working and start living on your retirement income. You may want to consider declaring bankruptcy. If you need more information about bankruptcy, go to the website at www.clearbankrupcy.com.

Putting It all Together

If you're fortunate enough to have a pension plan at work, make sure you know how much money you'll get and when you'll get it. Ease back on any risky investments that you might have retirement accounts and review your portfolio to see if your investments still meet your total needs. Know when you want to take your Social Security and remember you must apply for Medicare health insurance at age 65.

Don't assume that your taxes will be lower once you retire and stop earning taxable wages because that may not always be the case. The total of the monthly income needs to be less than the monthly expense and the non-monthly expense prorated to a monthly amount to be financially comfortable in retirement. And if you have paid off the mortgage, it could present you with an opportunity to leverage the equity into a smaller home. If cutting back on what you're spending doesn't make a big enough dent to help you make ends meet, you may need to make some hard choices now, before you retire.

You can head off the biggest fear by saving enough money to retire comfortably. Make sure you get a copy of our book, *Caution! Get Out of Debt Baby* that's available at www.Westernpubs.com. Charles Schwab's website will help you develop a retirement ready plan with their online calculators. Go to their home page at www.schwab.com and click on Advice & Retirement at the top of the menu.

Chapter 8

Putting Everything Together

Make sure you have all the parts when you put everything together

Assuming that you now know how much you'll need to retire, take a deep breath, and relax if the amount you'll need was higher than what you expected. Many people assume they'll have to work five or ten years longer than they had planned to build up enough money to retire. But a recent study by Financial Engines (www.financialengines.com) found that big loses or poor returns on investment don't necessarily translate into declines in projected retirement income. For many, paying off their home mortgages can get them back on course with careful planning. Most of us should be able to create the retirement we desire. Deciding when to retire should be more than just a matter of money. Much of the decision depends on what you want to do after you retire like traveling, starting a new avocation, or volunteer for a worthwhile cause.

Retirement is an opportunity to do things you never could find the time for. It is a chance to plan how to spend your next 50 years. But to take advantage of the retirement opportunity, you have to plan and prepare. Most of all, you need to know the new rules of retirement planning. We stand at the threshold of a transformation. The population is aging, and that is going to force us to reinvent retirement. We have seen the beginnings of this new retirement, but the real changes are coming in the next few years.

Another consideration is your health. As we get older, we're all naturally more susceptible to a greater variety of illnesses and physical limitations. If all you plan to do is sit out on the back porch whittling for the next 20 years, diminishing physical capability may not be all that much of an issue. But if your plans take in more active pursuits you'll want to be in adequate shape to get the most out of them. That, too, should enter into your thinking as to when the optimal retirement target might be.

You should be prepared to save more and to take investing more seriously than past retirees. You might not receive as much help from Social Security, Medicare, and your former employers as prior retirees did. Retirement might come gradually. Some simple steps are to work past age 65, invest a bit differently, save more, and plan for health care expenses. First, you might elect to take might be a reduction in hours worked. This may be followed by a gradual reduction in work-related activities until you take full retirement.

Owning a home that is paid for is a strategy that deserves special consideration because it can work for you during all the ups and downs of the economic cycle. During inflationary periods, home values typically go up at rates that stay even or beat inflation. Cooling home markets due to the recession and more stringent mortgage qualification standards have dropped the average prices of homes in many areas. If you don't own a home, it may be time to consider buying one.

Here's why a paid-off home is a smart investment strategy. They offer one of the best tax shelters (i.e., property tax and mortgage interest deductions) there is and if you work it right, a home that is paid off when you retire can become the anchor in your retirement plan. Microsoft's website (www.realestate.msn.com) covers every step of the home buying and owning process from researching neighborhoods to applying for a mortgage. The site also allows you to visit over 500,000 listings throughout the country. If you're handy with tools and a pain roller, consider buying a fixer-upper that may be priced 20 or 30 percent below the market.

Look for distress situations where the seller has to put a house on the market for a quick sale because of a foreclosure, job transfer, a divorce, or to settle an estate. Never be reluctant to submit an offer that is substantially less than the asking price. If your realtor balks, get another one. If you can, buy the cheapest house in the neighborhood because the higher-priced homes tend to pull the value of the lower-priced home up as they appreciate.

Appendix A

Glossary of Terms

401(k) plan is a broad label for a variety of employer-sponsored retirement savings incentive programs.

403(b) plan is a retirement plan available to employees of public schools, nonprofit organizations, or the clergy. It is identical to the 401(k), except that employers need not contribute, and they aren't subject to 401(k)'s stringent Employee Retirement Income Security Act (ERISA).

457 deferred-compensation plan sometimes called a deferred-camp plan, this retirement plan defers an employee's pay by the amount contributed, a characteristic shared by 401(k) and SIMPLE plans.

Account aggregator is an online platform that presents data from multiple accounts in a single interface that stores log-in information and simplifies web access to personal financial information.

Accrual method is an accounting method often used by businesses with inventory; with this method, you report income and deduct expenses when the work's done (you've done all the things you have to do to get paid and all the expenses have been incurred).

Active management is an investment management style that presumes that investments guided by a fund manager and informed by industry and economic insight should perform better than other similar investments.

Adjusted gross income (AGI) is the amount of income calculated by adding work income and other income such as investment interest and dividends or alimony. It excludes such things as alimony paid and the cost of health insurance paid by the self-employed.

Administrative fees are the fees that cover the cost of running the plan itself, including expenses such as the cost of preparing annual reports, running required discrimination tests, and supporting the website and customer service department.

Advertising is a means of informing the public about your product or service.

After-tax contributions are contributions to an IRA that is not deductible from a filer's tax obligation.

Age Discrimination in Employment Act was passed in 1967 and prohibits any employer from refusing to hire, discharge, or discriminate in any way based on a person's age.

Alternative minimum tax was created to close loopholes that enabled some super-rich taxpayers to pay unfairly low or even no taxes by resorting to legal tax shelters. Unfortunately, the tax lacks indexes to inflation, making more middle-class families vulnerable to assessment.

Angels are private investors willing to lend money or equity capital in much the same way as venture capitalists, but on a much smaller scale.

Annual expense ratio is the percentage of plan assets that are paid to cover operating, management, and marketing costs.

Annuity is a financial contract. You buy an annuity with the guarantee that the company-usually an insurance company-will provide a series of regular, fixed payments in exchange. Annuities come in a variety of forms.

Asset allocation is an investment recipe for all an individual's accounts, dictating the percentage of a portfolio invested in stocks, bonds, or cash.

Assisted living is a kind of housing that provides a modest amount of assistance, including bathing, dressing, and cooking meals.

Baby boomers are people born in a flourish of family-boosting activity that followed World War II and continued into the 1960s.

Balance sheet is a listing of assets, liabilities, and an owner's investment in a business as of a fixed date, such as the end of a quarter or year.

Basis is the amount you paid for property (called cost basis) or other amount treated as your investment in property. Adjusted basis is basis increased by additions or improvements and decreased by depreciation.

Benchmark is a standard used to compare performance, such as the Standard and Poor's 500 Index.

Blog is a web log that can be a marketing tool to express your political gripes, position you as an expert, and draw interest to your website.

Board and care is a type of assisted living that generally offers group meals and other activities for residents who want to spend time with friends and neighbors.

Bonds are a form of loan. In buying a bond, you're effectively entering into a contract with the issuer of that bond to pay whatever money you invested, plus interest. Bonds come in a variety of forms.

Book value is the real value of a company. It's calculated by totaling all assets and subtracting debt and liabilities.

Broadband service is a technology that allows the Internet connection to your computer to run faster and better.

Brochure ware is a website that functions like a written brochure, listing your product or services, rates, and contact information.

Business opportunity is a non-franchise arrangement in which you buy a concept for a product or service.

Business plan is a written report describing what a business is all about and where the business is heading in the future.

C Corporation is organized under state law and taxed as a separate person, but treated as a regular corporation.

Call provision are bonds that are paid off prior to their prearranged maturity.

Capital gain tax rate is the percentage of investing profits that must be paid in taxes, calculated as a proportion of the profit or capital gain of an investment.

Career average plans are similar to final pay programs, but based on the average of all the years you work for a company. You may get a percentage of your salary for every year you were in the plan. In other cases, you may get an average for all years you were in the plan.

Cash flow cycle time is the time over which inventory is ordered, paid for, sold, and money is received.

Cash method is an accounting method often used by service businesses. With this method, you record income when your client pays you and deduct expenses as they come up.

Cash value life insurance is a form of life insurance that builds accompanying cash value. These come in several different forms.

Catastrophic coverage is health insurance with exceedingly high deductibles.

Certificates of Deposits (CDs) are a form of promissory note; the lender effectively promises to pay you a certain interest rate if you let them hold your money for a specified amount of time.

COBRA (Consolidated Omnibus Budget Reconciliation Act) requires companies with 20 or more employees to allow you to stay on your health plan for an additional 18 months after you leave your job.

Cohousing is a semi-communal living arrangement where separate living units are arranged around a "common house."

Compounding is the effect of money earning interest which, in turn, results in a larger sum that earns even more.

Congregate housing is a variant of assisted living, offering both a level of assisted care as well as private living space.

Continuing care retirement communities involves several types of housing and living arrangements, including independent living facilities, assisted living, and nursing homes. Retirees can remain in the same retirement community, with the option to change the level of care they receive as their individual needs mandate it.

Conventional IRA was the first Individual Retirement Account introduced and defers any tax impact until you begin to withdraw money from the account.

Custodian is the institution that holds your IRA. It can be a bank, brokerage house, or similar place.

Certificate of deposit is a bank's promissory note to repay the amount deposited, with interest, at a future date, typically one month to five years away.

Chat rooms are locations on the Internet in which people interact with each other on a particular topic or area of mutual interest.

Cliff vesting is a vesting schedule in which none of an employer's contribution becomes an asset of the employee until the employee reaches a specified work anniversary. At the anniversary date, the employer's full contribution belongs to the employee.

Closely held corporation is a privately owned corporation whose stock is not traded on any public exchange.

Collection agency is a business that performs collection services, including sending reminders to late payers and suing delinquents on your behalf.

Commercial loan is money borrowed from a bank or other financial institution that specializes in business lending.

Compound interest is an investment principal in which interest is paid not only on the principal saved but also on the accumulated interest from prior periods that has not been withdrawn.

Constructive receipt is the date when income is treated as having been received by cash-basis businesses because it's under their control, even if they don't actually have the cash in hand (a check is income when received even though you haven't deposited or cashed it yet).

Contribution is an amount of cash or other assets deposited in a retirement account.

Cost of goods sold is the cost of inventory items such as materials, labor, and packaging.

Debt is borrowed money for financing a business. The borrower is called the debtor; the lender is called the creditor.

Deductible for insurance purposes is the amount of damage or liability that the insurance company won't cover. For taxes, it's the amount of expenses you can subtract against income.

Deep discount broker is an investment house that sells stocks and funds very inexpensively.

Defined benefit program is a pension payout based on your salary and number of years of service.

Defined contribution program is a program in which money is automatically deducted from your salary before you take possession of it. From there, the money is put into an investment vehicle of your choosing, including mutual funds, company stock, and other options.

Depreciation is a deduction of a portion of the cost of a car or other equipment you own over the life of the equipment (the life is set by the IRS) to reflect its true value.

Direct rollover is a process that directly transfers assets from one retirement plan into another.

Disability insurance provides income if you become disabled or temporarily unable to earn a living.

Discount brokers charge less than full-service brokers to execute trades.

Dividends are payments to shareholders authorized by a company's board of directors. They can be in cash or additional shares of the company's stock.

Dollar cost averaging is a savings strategy involving investing the same dollar amount at fixed intervals. If share prices increase, fewer shares are bought or if they decrease, more shares are bought at the different intervals.

Domain name is the address n the Internet where people can find your website.

Dow Jones Industrials is a stock index made up of 30 of the largest publicly held companies traded on the New York Stock Exchange.

Dying intestate is the legal term that refers to lack of a will or trust that provides instructions after someone dies.

ECHO is an acronym for Elder Cottage Housing Opportunities. This is usually a separate, small manufactured home that is added onto the side or backyard of an existing home.

Employee stock ownership plan (ESOP) is a program that allows employees to buy company stock, often with little or no commission.

Employer identification number is the number assigned to a business owner by the IRS after you file IRS Form SS-4. This is used for identification purposes on tax returns, bank accounts, and retirement plans.

Endorsement is a correction or change to an existing insurance policy.

Entrepreneur is someone who organizes and directs a start-up business, assuming the risk in the hope of making a profit.

Equity is the value of your home after subtracting the mortgage balance.

Equity financing a business happens when you bring investors in as part owners of the business.

Escrow is an arrangement in which a third party holds funds; when certain conditions are met, the funds are paid out.

Exchange traded funds (ETFs) are pooled investment accounts that resemble mutual funds in that they hold a basket of many individual investments but are traded directly on the stock exchanges by investors buying and selling their shares like stocks.

Expense ratio takes in all expenses incurred by a fund's operations and expresses them in terms of percentages.

Face value is the principal; the amount of money you invested when you bought a bond. It's also known as par value.

Fair market value is what a willing buyer and willing seller would pay, if neither is being forced to buy or sell and each understands all the facts and circumstances of the deal.

Fee for service is a form of health insurance that lets you choose any doctor or health care provider you like. Generally, the coverage pays 80 percent of any costs you accumulate.
You are obligated to pick up the remaining 20 percent.

Fee-only financial planner is a financial advisor who charges only for his advice, based on the consultation duration or project scope, and who doesn't sell investment products for commission in order to avoid conflict of interest in investment choice recommendations.

FICA (Federal Insurance Contributions Act) is the Social Security and Medicare taxes on wages paid by both the employer and the employee.

Final pay plan is a pension that can offer the biggest payout, as they average your salary over the last several years you're employed at a company.

Financial statement is information about income, expenses, sales figures, and other number-oriented items such as a cash flow statement, balance sheet, or profit and loss statement.

Fixed annuity is a tax deferred financial instrument marketed by insurance companies and brokerage firms that pays a fixed rate of interest that readjusts annually. Fixed Annuities are similar to CDs in that they pay a fixed rate of interest that readjusts on a yearly basis. Annuities are sold by life insurance companies and some brokerage firms.

Flat benefit plan is one of the most simple and straightforward pension payout. You receive a set monthly amount based on how long you worked for a company.

Flexible spending account is a program that allows you to set aside money from your salary tax-free. These funds can then be used to help pay for medical expenses that are not covered by your employer's health plan.

Franchise is a business arrangement that gives you the right to sell a product or service in a particular area. The company selling the concept is the franchisor; you are the franchisee. The right to a large territory is called a master franchise.

Fulfillment company is a business that takes and processes orders for you, including acceptance of payment by credit card. Generally, a fulfillment company charges a flat fee.

Full retirement age is the age at which you can receive your full retirement benefit from Social Security.

Fund family is several different mutual funds that a company maintains and offers to clients. The funds are usually set up for different financial objectives.

Fundamental analysis is a stock analysis involving examination of a company's operating statistics and numbers.

FUTA (Federal Unemployment Tax Act) is the Federal unemployment insurance tax paid by an employer on an employee's wages.

Goodwill is a favorable reputation of a business, which is considered an intangible asset.

Graded vesting is a vesting schedule in which an employer's contribution vests gradually over time, in stages or grades.

Grants are money from government sources or private foundations to start or run a business that matches the goals of the grant maker; grant money doesn't have to be repaid. .

Gross income is income before deductions. For purposes of the home office deduction, gross income means money from business minus expenses that don't relate to the use of the home such as office supplies or the salary of an employee.

Guaranteed investment contracts (GICs) is a contract involving a guaranteed rate of return.

Hobby loss rules are the tax rules that prevent an individual from deducting business expenses that are greater than business income where there's no reasonable expectation of making a profit from the business.

Home equity line of credit is a loan secured by the amount of equity you have in your home.

Home-office deduction is the total of deductions from the business use of a home office, including depreciation on the office or a portion of rent, as well as the portion of utilities and insurance related to the home office.

HTML (Hypertext Markup Language) is the programming language used on computers to create websites.

Independent contractor is a person who contracts to provide work according to his own methods. This person isn't under the control of the person or business for which the work is being performed (not an employee).

Income tax rate is the percentage of one's income that must be paid to local, state, or federal government.

Individual retirement accounts (IRA) are planned accounts that carry a tax advantage intended to encourage savings.

Individual 401(k) is a retirement savings program best suited for someone who works on their own and has no plans to bring on any employees in the future.

Inflation is the effect of rising prices on the value of money to buy goods and services.

Irrevocable trust is a trust that can't be changed in any way during the grantor's lifetime.

Internet is a worldwide collection of computer networks that you can access with a computer, modem, telephone line, and an online service provider or Internet service provider.

Invoice is an itemized list of products you've sold to someone, stating the quantity, price, and terms of sale; a bill for services rendered.

IRA basis is the amount contributed to an IRA that isn't eligible for tax deduction.

IRA trustee fees are costs paid by the investor that can include sales commissions, management fees, and marketing fee.

Joint and several liabilities is a legal rule that makes two or more parties fully responsible for damages, debt repayment, and other legal obligations.

Keogh plan is a tax-deferred retirement plan that lets small business owners and the self-employed save money for retirement.

Lifestyle funds are investment pools that resemble target-date funds in that they are a mix of mutual funds in an asset allocation that the mutual fund company chooses but that cater to risk tolerances.

Limited liability company is a type of business organization formed under state law that gives owners protection from personal liability but treats them as a partnership for tax purposes.

Limited partnership is a partnership in which one or more partners has limited personal liability and can't participate in the day-to-day operations of the business.

Limit orders is a stock purchase system that lets you establish prices at which you wish to buy or sell.

Living will also known as an advanced medical directive, this is a document that outlines your decisions about any sort of life-sustaining treatment.

Long-term care insurance is insurance you buy to pay for nursing home care and other sorts of long-term, comprehensive care.

Managed care also known as health maintenance organizations, is less expensive than fee for service. However, you have a limited choice of health care providers.

Medicaid is the federal program designed to pay for health care for the poor.

Medicare is the federal medical care program for persons age 65 and up. It is subdivided into four parts, offering different forms of coverage.

Medigap insurance is supplemental insurance to cover any gaps in Medicare coverage.

Marginal tax rate is the rate on the highest bracket a taxpayer's income reached.

Marketing is how people advertise, publicize, or otherwise inform each other of their product or service with the goal of exchanging products or services with each other.

Matching contribution is the employer plan-match option under which an employer promises to match a certain percentage of each employee's contribution up to a specific percentage of their pay.

Medical IRA known as a health savings account is an individual retirement account in which account holders can deposit pretax money to pay for medical expenses.

Modified adjusted gross income known as modified AGI, is the adjusted gross income from an IRA withdrawal by someone age

59½ or older, disabled or deceased, using the withdrawals to pay for college or other qualified higher education expenses, or using withdrawals toward
a first-time home purchase.

Money market deposit account is an investment account that often pays lower interest than a CD, but whose assets are accessible anytime without waiting for a future maturity date.

Money market fund is an investment account whose the cash in the account is accessible at anytime.

Monte Carlo calculator is a calculator that generates a measure of the probability that a given investment outcome scenario will result in a financially comfortable retirement based on expected assets, probable lifetime, and economic conditions.

Mutual funds are a combination of individual investments such as stocks, bonds, and cash bundled together into one product.

Net operating losses are business expenses in excess of business income; business losses that can be carried back 2 years and forward 20 years; also called NOLs.

Net unrealized appreciation is the difference in value between the average cost that you paid for stock and its current market value.

Network marketing is direct sales to consumers with distributors getting money from both direct sales and a percentage of the direct sales of other distributors they bring into the network.

Networking is word-of-mouth marketing in which contacts are made to try to drum up business.

Nonretirement accounts are bank or mutual fund accounts that are not held inside IRAs and on which taxes must be paid as accrued.

Overhead is the cost of monthly expenses, including electricity, telephone, insurance, and salaries of employees.

Partnership occurs when two or more people working together in a business with the intention of making a profit.

Passive management is an investment management style that seeks to match the market's performance.

Personal service corporation is subject to special tax rules; corporation engaged in the fields of health, law, accounting, engineering, architecture, actuarial science, performing arts, or consulting that meets certain ownership and service tests.

Plan provider is the company hired by an employer to administer their retirement plan, who often acting as the plan's trustee as well.

Points represent an up-front interest payment to a lender. One point is equivalent to 1 percent of the amount borrowed.

Power of attorney allows someone to make decisions when you're incapable of doing so yourself. Examples include medical and financial power of attorney.

Pretax contribution to a tax deferred retirement amount that a filer is permitted to deduct from their tax obligation.

Price-earnings ratio (PIE) is a popular stock ratio that illustrates how much an investor would be willing to spend in return for $1 in company earnings.

Price/book ratio (PIB) is a ratio that compares a stock's price to what a company is worth.

Price/sales ratio (P/S) is ratio that is calculated by dividing a current stock price by a company's earnings per share.

Primary insurance amount (PIA) is all your Social Security cash benefits, including your monthly benefit as well as benefits for dependents and survivors.

Probate is the legal process that the state must go through should you die with property still in your name.

Prime rate is the interest rate banks charge their preferred customers.

Profit sharing contribution is an employer contribution to their employees' retirement account that is made based on the profits of the company.

Promotion is the act of stimulating an immediate sale with special offers, such as discount coupons.

Publicly held corporation issues stock that is traded on a public exchange such as the New York Stock Exchange.

QUADRO is a divorce-specific transfer between two people's accounts requiring a court order.

Qualified is a term that means a pension program has to adhere to certain governmental guidelines for tax purposes.

Real estate investment trusts (REITs) are funds that invest in property, including shopping centers, apartment buildings, and similar commercial operations.

Rebalancing are adjustments to an asset allocation that correct for different assets having performed differently over time, eventually comprising different portfolio percentages than intended.

Reverse mortgage is a mortgage that lets you tap the accumulated equity in your home. In doing so, your loan balance increases rather than going down.

Revocable trust is a trust that may be changed or eliminated completely.

Rider is an additional clause to an existing contract or insurance policy to cover a special item or event (usually an upgrade to a policy); sometimes referred to as an endorsement.

Risk tolerance is the amount of uncertainty and volatility with which an investor feels comfortable.

Roth 401(k) is an employer-sponsored retirement account in which tax liability accrues upon contribution but whose account earnings and withdrawals are tax-free.

Roth 403(b) is an employer-sponsored retirement account offered to employees of public schools, nonprofit organizations, and the clergy in which tax liability accrues upon contribution but whose account earnings and withdrawals are tax-free.

Roth IRA is a form of individual retirement account in which taxes do not accrue on withdrawn funds, whether earnings or basis.

S Corporation also called a Subchapter S Corporation is organized under state law that elects to have business income taxed to its shareholders.

Safe-harbor 401(k) is an employee-sponsored plan that reduces an employer's effort and cost in running the plan's nondiscrimination tests.

SBA (Small Business Administration) is a federal agency that sponsors loan programs and other assistance to small businesses.

SBICs (Small Business Investment Companies) are privately managed firms licensed by the SBA to make loans to small businesses.

Search engines are websites that enable you to find other pages on the web, just like a library card catalog helps you find books on shelves.

Self-employment tax is Social Security and Medicare taxes paid by self-employed individuals, such as sole proprietors, on their net earnings from the business.

Self-insured is having sufficient assets to make life insurance unnecessary.

SEP plan known as the Simplified Employee Pension plan is a retirement option popular with people who are self-employed and who don't have employees in which 100 percent of the contributions come from the employer.

Shareholders are the owners of a corporation (also called stockholders) whose ownership interest is in the form of stock certificates.

Shares outstanding are the total number of shares owned by an investor.

SIMPLE 401(k) plan is a plan that combines the features of SIMPLE IRAs and regular 401(k) plans, including contribution limits and employer match rules of SIMPLE plans.

SIMPLE IRA is an acronym for Savings Incentive Match Plan. This type of IRA is particularly suited to someone whose self-employment income is relatively modest-$30,000 annually or less.

SIMPLE Plan also known as the Savings Incentive Match Plan for Employees is a common option in companies with 30 or fewer employees but available to companies with up to 100 employees, an IRA account into which both employee and employer can contribute.

Simplified Employee Pensions is retirement plan available to employers and the self-employed. All contributions are tax-deductible.

Single-person 401(k) also called a solo 401(k) and a self-employed 401(k) is a retirement plan that simplifies the administration of a

401(k) enough to make it affordable for single-person companies and very small enterprises.

Sixty-day rollover is a transfer of assets from a 401(k) plan to an individual retirement account during a 60-day period and that assesses a 10 percent early withdrawal penalty unless the rollover is not completed in 60 days.

Social Security formally known as the Federal Old Age, Survivors and Disability Insurance program provides retirement funding and other benefits to participants.

Sole proprietorship is an unincorporated business owned by one person.

Solution providers are companies that provide all-in-one packages for running an online business (usually for a flat monthly fee).

Start-up phase is the period in which a business begins operation, generally the first three months.

Stock is a share of ownership in a company. Stocks come in a variety of types, with different features and objectives.

Stop loss orders is a method of stock buying specifically designed to limit your losses and protect whatever profit you may have earned from a stock.

Summary Plan Description (SPD) is the book of rules that governs your specific 401(k) plan, including when an employee will be eligible to participate and the specifics about how to contribute to the account and how money can be withdrawn.

Surrender value is the amount you receive if you cash out a life insurance policy.

Target date fund is a mutual fund whose allocation of assets are tailored to perform best within a time specific event, like your retirement date.

Tax credit is a reduction in income tax on a dollar-for-dollar basis.

Tax deferred is the income gains generated by investments that do not become taxable until the funds are withdrawn from the account.

Tax-deductible is the quality of income or capital gains generated by investments that can reduce tax liability by the amount deposited into a retirement account.

Taxable income is the earning from an individual's job and investments that are taxable each year.

Teaser cards are credit cards with very low interest rates that last only for a limited amount of time.

Technical analysis is a stock analysis on which a company's trading patterns are charted and analyzed.

Term life insurance is the simplest form of life insurance, as it involves no cash value.

Testamentary trust is a trust, created under a last will and testament that becomes effective only after the grantor dies and the will is admitted to probate.

Timing the market means determining at a particular moment in time, which way the market is going – up or down or sideways.

Treasury securities are issued and backed by the federal government. They come in various forms, including securities, notes, savings bonds, and other formats.

Trustee fees are the cost paid by investors in retirement accounts that can include sales commissions, management, and administration fees.

Trusts are a legal vehicle in which one person (known as the trustee) holds property for another person (known as the beneficiary). This trustee can be a person or a trust company. Trusts are useful in distributing the assets of an estate.

Turnkey business is a business that is ready to go into operation, with all materials, processes, and equipment in place to produce a product or service.

Umbrella insurance is an additional form of liability insurance coverage.

Unearned income is income you don't earn. Common examples are pension and annuity payouts, dividends, and interest and proceeds from life insurance.

URL (Uniform Resource Locator) is another name for a web address.

Value averaging is a variant on dollar-cost averaging that takes into account stock price movement.

Variance is a change or alteration of a zoning rule granted specifically for one person.

Venture capitalists are people or companies that invest in businesses (often technology related)
with the expectation of realizing big profits in the future.

Virtual workers are people who do jobs from their own locations, such as answering your telephone from their home offices rather than from your office.

Waiting period is the time between the onset of a disability and when benefits begin.

Will is a written document that delineates how you want your property distributed after you die.

Withdrawal is a cash value of an asset redeemed from a retirement account.

Work credits are a system to determine Social Security eligibility. You become formally eligible once you have accumulated 40 "work credits."

Yield is the effective rate of interest that a bond pays to investors.

Appendix B

Additional Information Sources

Annual Stock Reports

Investor Guide (*www.investorguide.com/stocklist.cgi*) provides links to thousands of publicly traded companies.

Best Calls *(www.bestcalls.com)* provides access to companies' quarterly earnings press conferences.

Public Register's Annual Report Service *(www.prars.com)* offers both online and hard copy annual reports.

Thomson Investor Net (*www.thomsoninvest.net*) covers more than 7,000 in-depth company reports that are updated twice a month.

Security Exchange Commission (SEC) is the official government site that hosts all financial reports of the publicly traded companies in the United States. Their website is at *www.sec.gov*.

Bonds

Bonds Online (*www.bondsonline.com*) provides charts and historical data that compare the various bond market sectors.

The Bond Market (*www.bondcan.com*) specializes in investing in Canadian bonds.

The Bond Market Association *(www.bondmarket.com)* is loaded with information about thousands of bonds and their respective trading history.

Brokers

Charles Schwab *(www.schwab.com)*

Fidelity Investments *(www.jidelity.com)*

T. Rowe Price *(www.troweprice.com)*

Vanguard Group *(www.vanguard.com)*

Budgeting

You can view a sample budget at *www.personalbudgeting.com*. A good resource for developing a budget is available at *www.simpleplanning.net*. The following websites contain good budget tools:

www.flexibleretirementplanner.com
www.smartmoney.com
www.money.com
www.personalbudgeting.com
www.simpleplanning.com
www.tdameritrade.com
www.fidelity.com/myplan

Credit Cards and Credit Scores

To find out about credit card options, visit *www.e-wisdom.com*. The website at *www.cardratings.com* offers a variety of resources to help you understand everything related to credit cards. For a fee, you can find out what your score is at *www.myjico.com*. You can check your credit report at all three bureaus at *www .annualcreditreport.com*. The following websites will provide you with additional information about credit cards and credit scores:

www.cardrating.com
www.cardratings.com
www.myfico.com
www.annualcreditreport.com

Debt Reduction

If you need more advice on reducing your debt, try Barnes & Noble's website *www.barnesandnoble.com)* or Amazon's website *(www.amazon.com)* and browse through their debt-related books. The website at *http://cgi.money.cnn.com/tools/debtplanner/debtplannerjsp* will help you project when you will be debt free. If you are interested in learning more about bankruptcy, go to *www.banhruptcvinfo.com.* Qpicken.com offers a Debt Reduction Planner, an excellent tool for about $50. The following websites will provide you with debt reduction information:

www.defeatthedebt.com
www.cgi.money.cnn.com
www.bankrupcyinfo.com
www.smartmoney.com
www.money.com
www.simpleliving.net
www.debetorsanonymous.org
www.clearbankrupcy.com

Discount Brokers

Accutrade *(www.accutrade.com) 800-494-8939*

American Express (*www.americanexpress.com*) 800-658-4677

Morgan Stanley *(www.morganstanley.com) 212-761-4000*

E*Trade *(www.etrade.com) 800-387-2331*

Fidelity *(wwwjidelity.com) 800-544-8666*

Muriel Siebert *(www.msiebert.com) 800-872-0444*

Schwab *(www.schwab.com) 800-435-4000*

Scottrade *(scottrade.com) 800-619-7283*

Wall Street Access *(www.wsaccess.com) 800-925-5782*

TD Ameritrade *(www.tdameritrade.com) 800-669-3900*

Diversified Investing

Legg Mason's website *(www.leggmason.com)* provides an online questionnaire to help you develop a diversification plan.

Frank Russell Company'{ *www.russell.com)* features a Comfort Quiz to help you allocate your investments.

Fidelity's Asset Diversification Planner *(www.fidelity.com)* offers diversification advice, a risk questionnaire, and model portfolios.

The Intelligent Asset Allocator *(www.eJficientfrontier.com)* offers comprehensive information on how to build a diversified portfolio.

Education

To learn more about federal financial aid for college and how to apply, visit the U.S. Department of Education's website at *www.ed.gov.*

The American Association of Individual Investors offers advice on funds and portfolio management on their website at *www.aaii.com.*

Bloomberg Personal Finance *(www.bloomberg.com)* offers online training when you click on the Bloomberg University module.

Investing Basics *(www.aaii.com/invbas)* offers feature articles about how to start successful investment programs, pick winning stocks, and evaluate your options.

Investor Guide *(www.investorguide.com)* features more than 1,000 answers to frequently asked questions.

Money 101 provides an interactive investment seminar at *www.money.cnn.com*. Money's *www.eldernet.comlmoney.htm* offers tutorials and advice on investing in stocks, mutual funds, and bonds.

Morningstar's University (*www.morningstar.com*) offers a comprehensive investment education program. The Motley Fools offer an investment seminar on their website at *www.fool.com*.

The Mutual Fund Education Alliance is the trade association for no-load funds and offers advice on how to select funds *(www.mfea.com)*.

Vanguard *(www.vanguard.com)* offers online courses that cover the fundamentals of investing in mutual funds.

Estate Planning

If you want to create a basic will on your computer, Quicken offers a software product called Will Maker that is available in computer stores and at *www.nolo.com*. The following websites will provide you with additional estate planning information:

www.quicken.com
www.nolo.com
www.smartmoney.com
www.money.com
www.kinplinger.com
www.smartmoney.com/retirement
www.mpower.com
www.financialengines.com
www.morningstar.com

Financial Calculators

www.kinplinger.com
www.socialsecurity.gov/estimator
www.fincalc.com
www.dinkytown.com
www.calc.xml

www.dinkytown.com
www.riskgrades.com
www.choosetosave.org/calculators
www.schwab.com
www.troweprice.com

Financial and Economic News

The Bureau of Economic Analysis *(www.bea.gov)* calculates economic indicators such as the gross domestic product and other regional, national, and international data, all of which are displayed on their website.

Census Bureau *(www. census.gov)* provides information about industry statistics and general business conditions.

STAT-USA *(www.stat-usa.gov)* is sponsored by the U.S. Department of Commerce and provides financial information about economic indicators, statistics, and economic news.

Financial Planning Organizations

The American Institute of Certified Public Accountants *(www.aicpa.org)*
Personal Financial Planning Division, 1211 Avenue of the Americas, New York, NY 10036, 800-862-4272

The National Association of Personal Financial Advisors *(www. nap/a. org)* 355 W. Dunbee Rd., Suite 200, Buffalo Grove, IL 60089, 800-333-6659

A website that offers a variety of articles on financial planning is at *ww.money.cnn.com.*

Financial Publications and News Sites

www.money.cnn.com
www.cnnmoney.com
www.simpleplanning.com

www.fidelity.com
www.businessweek.com
www.kinplinger.com
www.morningstar.com
www.kiplinger.com
www.Yodlee.com
www.investools.com
www.quicken.com
www.fidelity.com
www.Smartinvestmentbook.com

Financial Tools

The Financial Center *(wwwfinancia!center.com)* has a section for retirees. Choose United States and then financial planning. Under this category, choose retirement. Schwab *(www.schwab.com)* helps you develop a financial plan with its online calculators, tools, and advice. Virtual Stock Exchange by Market Watch *(www.virtualstock exchange.com)* is a stock-simulation game that allows you to trade shares just as you would in a real brokerage account.

Government Agencies

www.irs.gov
www.irs.gov
www.completetax.com
www.medicare.gov
www.socialsecurity.gov/estimator
www.socialsecurity.gov

Home Based Businesses

U.S. Small Business Administration (800) 827-5722; *sba.gov*
American Home Business Association (866) 396-7773 homebusinessworks.com
Entrepreneur.com is an online small business resource center providing information and advice on products, services and resources.

Familybusinessmagazine.com offers tips, articles and advice about starting and operating a family business.

Home-based-business-opportunities.com features hundreds of home based and small business opportunities listings.

Homebusinessmag.com is an online magazine with information, advice, tools and links for home business owners.

Powerhomebiz.com provides information, advice and tools for home business owners.

Sbomag.com is the Small Business Opportunities Magazine providing readers with the latest small business opportunities news, information and industry resources.

Index Funds

There are literally hundreds of mutual funds that index every segment of the market. Here are two of the better funds to consider: Fidelity Spartan Market Index Fund, which mirrors the Standard & Poor's 500 (S&P 500) index (800-544-8888) T. Rowe Price Equity Index Fund mirrors the S&P 500 (800-638-5660).

Industry Trends

ABC News *(www.abcnews.com)* features articles on current industry news and market expert commentary. American Society of Association Executives *(www.asaenet.org)* provides high quality industry overviews including briefings of industry trends. Hoovers Online *(www.stockscreener.com)* offer excellent information on industries at their website. *Research* magazine *(www.researchmag.com)* offers helpful references to industry news, columns, and highlights.

Insurance

If you are paying for your own health insurance, go to *www.ehealthinsurance.com*to determine if there is a less expensive plan to switch to. The website at *www.nmfn.com* will help you estimate your life span and need for life insurance based on your age, gender, lifestyle, and medical history.

International Investing

The Internet is rich in sources for information on foreign companies. Three websites in particular with useful information are *www.bankofny.com,* *wwwjpmorgan.com,* and *www.global-investor.com.* Also, FT Market Watch *(wwwftmarketwatch.com)* provides up-to-the minute news on offshore companies and foreign markets.

Investment Advice

The websites at *www.morningstar.com, www.kiplinger.com,* and *www.investools.com* will help you select stocks and mutual funds that meet your investment parameters. Shop around for the best certificate of deposit rates in your area at *www.bankrate.com.* To learn more about home loans, foreclosure prevention, and predatory lending, go to *www.loansafe.org.* Bankrate.com can find the best rates available in your area for motor vehicles. Bank of America's website *(www.bankamerica.com)* offers a retirement center under the heading Achieve Your Goals on their main menu. It has several useful references for advice for retirees. Investor Home *(www.investorhome.com)* provides information about the investment process and how to bulletproof your portfolio.

Investment Associations

American Association of Individual Investors *(www.aaii.com)* offers a variety of valuable services to their members, including local chapter meetings in the major metropolitan areas. The National Association of Investors Corporation (NAIC) is a national association with local chapters throughout the country. Their goal is to help investors develop a disciplined approach to successful investing. For more information, visit their website at *www.better-investing.org.*

Magazines

Business Week(www.businessweek.com) is available online to all of its subscribers.

Forbes (www.forbes. com) is available online and features articles on personal finance and investing.

Fortune (wwwfortune.com) includes special market reports as well as stock and fund quotes.

Kiplinger's (www.kiplinger.com) has a broader scope than many of its competitors. Instead of talking just about investing, *Kiplinger's* moves into other issues of personal business, such as credit card spending, loans, college tuition, and vacation planning. For subscription information, call 800-624-2946.

Newsweek (www.newsweek.com) not only covers the general news but also covers the latest news about the stock market. *SmartMoney* is the" *Wall Street Journal* magazine of personal business" and it's excellent. For subscription information, call 800-444-4204 or visit their website at *www.smartmoney.com.*

Worth columnists, including Peter Lynch, are second to none, and the magazine's regular features are dynamite. For subscription information, call 800-777-1851 or go to www.*worth com. Money* does an excellent job of keeping its readers informed about what's happening in the mutual fund market. For subscription information, visit their website at *www.money.com.*

Motor Vehicle Acquisition

For comprehensive car-buying information, go to *www.edmunds.com, www.autobytelcom,* and *www.carsmart.com.* To get an estimate of used car values, go to the Kelly Blue Book at *www.kbb.com.* Edmunds at *www.cdmunds.com* or eAuto at *www.eauto.com.* If you are interested in purchasing a new vehicle, check out *www.autosite.com* to find dealer invoice prices or find out about the maintenance records on cars that interest you. If you are interested in purchasing a used vehicle, check out:

Trader Online *(www.traderonline.com)*
 Kelley Blue Book's Classifieds *(www.kbb.com)*

Online Auto *(www.onlineauto.com)*
Auto Web Interactive *(www.autoweb.com)*.

Mutual Fund Companies and Brokers

Charles Schwab *(www.schwab.com)*
Fidelity Investments *(www.jidelity.com)*
T. Rowe Price *(www.troweprice.com)*
Vanguard Group *(www.vanguard.com)*

Mutual Funds

There are almost as many mutual funds to choose from as there are stocks. The following websites will help you find the best ones out there:

CBS Market Watch *(www.marketwatch.com)* provides articles, news, and market data on funds.

MaxFunds *(www.maxfunds.com)* specializes in offering news and statistics on small and little-known funds.

Morningstar *(www.morningstar.com)* is a premier site providing all kinds of information about mutual funds.

Fidelity *(wwwjidelity.com)* offers direct purchase plans for its funds.

Janus *(www.janus. com)* has a family of no-load funds that you can purchase or apply for online.

T. Rowe Price *(www.troweprice.com)* offers direct purchase plans for its funds.

Vanguard *(www.vanguard.com)* has more than eighty funds that you can purchase directly from the company.

News Online

One of the biggest advantages of getting your news online is that you can go to the specific news sector (e.g., Market Watch) without having to thumb through a bunch of paper to get there. Here are several excellent sites to try:

ABC News *(www.abcnews.com)* features business and industry news and market commentary.

Bloomberg Personal Finance *(www.bloomberg.com)* is loaded with timely business news, data, and an analysis of the market.

News Page *(www.newspage.com)* allows you to customize daily news abstracts that it sends to your e-mail address.

Newspapers

Financial newspapers are still a way of life in the stock market's paper-oriented world, although some of them are beginning to make the migration over to the online sector. Here's a rundown of several excellent papers that are out there:

The *Financial Times (wwwft.com)* provides special reports on the market and the different industry sectors.

Investor's Business Daily is a great financial newspaper that publishes important information to help determine the value of a stock. For subscription information, call 800-831-2525 or visit their website at *www.investors.com.*

The *New York Times (www.nytimes.com)* provides a business section that includes quotes and charts, a portfolio management tool, and breaking business news.

USA Today (www.usatoday.com) features a money section that includes investment articles and news, economic information, and information on industry groups.

The *Wall Street Journal* is the Big Kahuna among investment newspapers, although its authority isn't as unquestioned as it used to be. For subscription information, call 800-778-0840 or visit their website at *www.wsj.com*.

Portfolio Management

There are several portfolio management tools that you can use to manage your portfolio. Check out the following websites:

Morningstar (*www.morningstar.com*) provides a portfolio setup menu that is easy to use.

Quicken *(www.quicken.com)* offers a variety of financial tools including an excellent portfolio-management program.

Microsoft (*www.money.msn.com*) offers a wealth of financial data.

Professional Advice

The following websites will provide you with access to professional advisors:

www.napfa.org
www.fpanet.org
www.aicpa.org

Quotes (Stocks and Mutual Funds)

American Stock Exchange (*www.amex.com*) offers quoting services on their website for stocks that are traded on its exchange.

Microsoft Investor (*www.investor.msn.com*) offers a free stock ticker that you can personalize along with portfolio-tracking tools.

The National Association of Securities Dealers *(www. nasdaq.com)* offers quoting services on their website for stocks that are traded on its exchange.

The New York Stock Exchange *(www.nyse.com)* offers quoting services on their website for stocks that are traded on its exchange.

PC Quote *(www.pcquote.com)* offers current stock prices, portfolio tracker, company profiles, and broker recommendations.

Business Week (www.businessweek.com/investor) features applicable information for researching investment opportunities.

Real Estate

Cost-of-living and moving calculators are available at *http://cgi.money.cnn.com/tools*. To calculate mortgage rates and review *Money* magazine articles on real estate, go to *www.usatoday.comlmoney*. The following websites will provide you with additional information on real estate:

www.bankrate.com
www.realestate.msn.com
www.craigslist.com
www.wheretoretire.com

Reducing Expenses

www.carpoolworld.com
www.erideshares.com
www.campusbookretals.com
www.chegg.com
www.billshrink.com
www.energystar.gov

Retirement Planning

Charles Schwab's website will help you develop a retirement plan with their online calculators, tools, and advice at *www.schwab.com* (click on Advice & Retirement at the top of the menu).
Quicken offers a software product called Will Maker that is available at several computer stores and online at *www.nolo.com.* A

retirement budget worksheet is available at *wwwjidelity.com* when you select the Retirement & Guidance option in their main menu.

A retirement calculator can be accessed at *www.usnews.com* when you select the Retirement sub-menu that is under their Money & Business main menu. If you are interested in getting an annuity quote, go to *www.immediateannuities.com*. The following websites will provide you with additional information on retirement planning:

www.flexibleretirementPlanner.com
www.immediateannuities.com
www.quicken.com/retirment/planner
www.kinplinger.com
www.smartmoney.com
www.money.com
www.schwab.com
60 Plus Association at *www.60plus.org*
American Association of Retired People at *www.aarp.org*
Fifty Plus at *www.fifty-plus.net*
Grand Times at *www.grandtimes.com*
Hoover's Online *(www.stockscreener.com)* provides a special module for retirement planning
Information Seniors at *www.infoseniors.com*

Reverse Mortgages

www.aarp.com
www.revmort.com/nrmla

Savings Programs

For steps to take to save money, go to *www.themoneykeys.com*. To determine if you are saving enough, go to *www.kiplinger.com*

Shopping and Selling

If you are shopping for an item or selling an item that would be difficult to get an appraisal on, see what similar items are selling for in the classified advertisements or on *www.ebay.com, www.netmarket.com,* or *www.craigslist.com.* Yellow Page listings are available at *http://search.bigfoot.com* or *www.switchboard.com.* The following websites will provide you with additional information on shopping and buying on the internet:

www.bluefly.com
www.yoox.com

Stock and Mutual Fund Market Timing

The following websites will provide you with additional information on timing the stock and mutual fund markets:

www.schwab.com
www.trowprice.com
vanguard.com
www.fidelity.com
www.fundalarm.com
www.timingthemarket.net
www.stockcharts.com
www.vectorvest.com

Stock Evaluation Programs

Finding out what stock analysts are saying about a stock that you're considering can help you determine if it's the right time to buy. Here are several sites that will get you the information you need:

VectorVest *(www.vectorvest.com)* offers free reports showing what your stocks are really worth, how safe they are, and when to buy, sell, or hold. It's one of the best analyst's sites on the Internet.

S&P Advisor Insight *(www.advisorinsight.com)* allows you to review Standard & Poor's reports for major stocks.

Zacks Investment Research *(www.zacks.com)* reports on what analysts are saying about most of the stocks on the U.S. exchanges.

Stock Exchanges

The American, NASDAQ and New York Stock Exchanges offer a wide variety of investment features that may appeal to you.

American Stock Exchange *(www.amex.com)*
The National Association of Securities Dealers *(www. nasdaq.com)*
The New York Stock Exchange *(www.nyse.com)*.

Taxes

For tax deductions, go to *www.bottomlinesecrets.comlextra*. For tax preparation ideas, go to *http://tax.yahoo.comlchecklist.html*.

Travel Websites

www.expedia.com
www.travelocity.com
www.besifares.com
www.budgettravel.com

Web Search Engines

Alta Vista: *www.altavista.com*
Google: *www.google.com*
HotBot: *www.hotbot.com*
Lycos: *uruno.lycos.com*
Yahoo!: *www.yahoo.com*

About The Author & Testimonials

David Rye was the founder of Computech Corporation and later, a director at IBM where he earned an MBA with honors from Seattle University. He is currently president of Western Publications and writes personal finance books from his Goodyear, Arizona office. His award-winning books include *It's Not Too Late To Rescue Your 401(k)*, *250 Questions To Ask before You Retire*, *Starting Up*, and *1001 Way to Inspire Yourself*. He also consultants baby boomers to show them how to get the most out of their retirement plans.

"Perfect for boomers who are about to retire and are thinking about retiring … in a standard of living they can be comfortable with."
Dr. T.K. Nelsen, Stanford University

"A great book in a writing style that is highly interactive where each chapter challenges to reader to expand their role in getting more out of their investments … you'll learn how you can retire in $tyle."
Dale Moser, President and CEO, Niwot Technology, Inc.

"A hands-on book that dramatically illustrates how anyone can enjoy financial freedom after they retire."
Mark Kruger, Ph.D., Creative Thinking Seminars

"… adds an element of real world reality to the retirement process that is truly unique and refreshing."
A.J. Osorio, President, Llanos Publishing

www.ingramcontent.com/pod-product-compliance
Lightning Source LLC
Chambersburg PA
CBHW051528170526

45165CB00002B/656